I Can See Tomorrow

I Can See Tomorrow

A Guide for Living with Depression

Patricia L. Owen, Ph.D.

With a foreword by Bert Pepper, M.D.

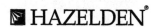 HAZELDEN®

Hazelden
Center City, Minnesota 55012-0176

Library of Congress Cataloging-in-Publication Data
Owen, Patricia L.
    I can see tomorrow : a guide for living with depression / Patricia L.
Owen ; with a foreword by Bert Pepper.
      p.   cm.
    Includes bibliographical references and index.
    ISBN 1-56838-087-9
    1. Depression, Mental—Popular works. I. Title.
RC537.094 1995
616.85'27—dc 20   95-30883
                                                      CIP

Editor's note

Hazelden offers a variety of information on chemical dependency and related areas. Our publications do not necessarily represent Hazelden's programs, nor do they officially speak for any Twelve Step organization.

The Twelve Steps are reprinted and adapted with permission of Alcoholics Anonymous World Services, Inc. Permission to reprint and adapt the Twelve Steps does not mean that Alcoholics Anonymous has reviewed or approved the contents of this publication, nor that AA agrees with the views expressed herein. The views expressed herein are solely those of the author. AA is a program of recovery from alcoholism. Use of the Twelve Steps in connection with programs and activities that are patterned after AA, but that address other problems, does not imply otherwise.

The Twelve Steps for Healing by Lewis Andrews, copyright 1992 by the Hazelden Foundation, are reprinted by permission of Hazelden.

All the stories in this book are based on actual experiences. The names and details have been changed to protect the privacy of the people involved. In some cases, composites have been created.

Contents

Foreword by Bert Pepper, M.D.   viii

Acknowledgments   xii

Introduction   1

1. What Is Depression?   5
   What Are the Types of Depression?   5
   Other Ways to Look at Depression?   10
   Common Threads of Depression   12
   What If I Am Recovering from Addiction?   13
   Is This Me?   14
   What Does This Mean for Me?   19
   Further Questions   20
   What Can I Do to Help Myself?   21

2. Who Has Depression?   23
   You Are Not Alone   23
   What If I Am Recovering from Addiction?   25
   What Does This Mean for Me?   26
   Further Questions   26
   What Can I Do to Help Myself?   27

3. What Causes Depression?   29
   Biological Factors   29

Contents

Environmental Factors   34

Associated Factors   37

What If I Am Recovering from Addiction?   48

What Does This Mean for Me?   49

Further Questions   49

What Can I Do to Help Myself?   51

4. What Can I Do About My Depression? Psychotherapy   55

What Is Psychotherapy?   55

How Do I Find a Therapist?   66

Is Psychotherapy Working? The Patterns of Change in Therapy   69

What If I Am Recovering from Addiction?   72

What Does This Mean for Me?   73

Further Questions   74

What Can I Do to Help Myself?   75

5. What Can I Do About My Depression? Antidepressant
    Medication   77

What Is Antidepressant Medication?   77

How Do I Decide Whether to Use Antidepressant Medication?   84

What Is It Like to Take Antidepressant Medication?   89

What Are the Side Effects of Antidepressant Medication?   93

When and How Do I Stop Taking Antidepressant Medication?   98

What If I Am Recovering from Addiction?   105

The Effect of Medications on Alcoholism/Addiction   113

What Does This Mean for Me?   117

Further Questions   120

What Can I Do to Help Myself?   127

6. Depression and the Family   129

The Importance of Family   129

What Does This Mean for Me?   131

Further Questions   132

What Can I Do to Help Myself?   133

7. Depression as a Spiritual Phenomenon   135
    Asking Spiritual Questions   136
    Recognizing When a Spiritual Journey Alone Cannot Help
       Depression   137
    Recognizing the Role of Depression   140
    What If I Am Recovering from Addiction?   146
    What Does This Mean for Me?   150
    Further Questions   151
    What Can I Do to Help Myself?   151

Appendix: A Brief Guide to Common Medications Used for
    Depression   153
    Selective Serotonin Re-Uptake Inhibitors and Other Newer
       Antidepressants   153
    Unique Antidepressants   156
    Tricyclic Antidepressants   158
    Monoamine Oxidase Inhibitors   164
    Mood Stabilizers   167

The Twelve Steps of Alcoholics Anonymous   169

Resources   170

Endnotes   171

Index   179

About the Author   185

Foreword

With this book on depression, Pat Owen, Ph.D., and I—a psychologist and psychiatrist, respectively—pursue our mutual interest: helping depressed people and their families help themselves heal by giving them the latest scientific information. We hope this book will lead many to the path of recovery, away from the dreadful rut of loneliness, sadness, hopelessness—away from *depression*.

This user-friendly book will help people who know they are experiencing depression. It will also help people who wonder if what they are experiencing is clinical depression, or if they are just feeling down because of a past or current problem with alcohol. It will help the reader sort out *whether* there is a depressive or other mood disorder, *what* might have caused it, and *how* help can be found. This is particularly important because depression, along with the anxiety disorders that frequently accompany it, increases the risk of suicidal thinking and behavior. And if alcohol is involved, the risk of suicide increases greatly.

Recent research clearly shows that many people whose depressive symptoms are not severe enough to warrant a diagnosis of clinical depression nevertheless lose the ability to experience full and joyous lives. This book includes information that is valuable for such people, as well as for those who have a more severe, diagnosable level of depression.

This book also discusses psychotherapy and antidepressants, and how they can be used together. Too many people who seek help go to *either* a psychiatrist *or* a psychologist or other therapist. In some cases the psychiatrist (an M.D.) may prescribe medication, but neglect the needed psychotherapy and family work; in other cases the nonmedical psychotherapist may do an excellent job of counseling, but neglect referral to, and joint work with, a cooperating psychiatrist. The result is that the client does not get all the benefits of modern treatment research, or medication, which could be extremely helpful.

This book introduces the reader to a balanced, integrated treatment approach, one that applies *biological, psychological,* and *social factors.* The result, I believe, is a practical volume that will be useful either as a self-help book or an adjunct to professional treatment.

Although my specialty in psychiatry is treating persons with depressive disorders, I am also deeply involved in the prevention and treatment of alcohol and drug abuse as self-medication for depression. It is therefore my hope that, in a curious way, this book may help some people avoid alcoholism. Here's how: left untreated, depression increases the risk of developing alcohol or other drug abuse. People turn to alcohol (self-medication) for temporary relief of their psychic and emotional pain. While alcohol can relieve depressive symptoms for a few hours, it is certainly no cure for the illness. Over time alcohol usually leads to greater depression. This is easy enough to understand: alcohol is a depressant.

Readers may wonder how a depressant drug like alcohol can temporarily relieve depressive symptoms. Current medical thinking says that alcohol depresses all functions of the brain and, indeed, all organs of the body. But in small doses, alcohol selectively depresses areas of the brain that function as centers of inhibition. In turn, the brain is allowed to be more active, to be *disinhibited*—a key part of intoxication.

Of course, we all know the effects of disinhibition: people say things that hurt the people they care about, they drive recklessly, and so on. For example, someone who is disinhibited may race a yellow light at an intersection. More than 50 percent of auto accidents and fatalities involve alcohol.

But feeling disinhibited may be quite pleasurable for the depressed person who is not an alcoholic. For instance, for the first time in a long time, the person may enjoy the companionship of friends. However, over time depressed people who drink find that they need to drink more to get the effect they want (this is even more so than for other social drinkers). This phenomenon is well known as *tolerance*—the body becomes accustomed to the alcohol and thus requires more alcohol to get the same effect.

As the depressed person—or anyone else developing tolerance—eventually discovers, something new happens when the dose of alcohol is increased to overcome tolerance and get that good, disinhibited feeling once again.

With increased amounts of alcohol, the effects are no longer limited to the inhibitory centers of the brain. The alcohol now depresses all areas of the brain, as well as the heart, lungs, digestive tract, and the other organs and tissues of the body. Further, while very small doses have not been shown to be toxic, medical research has proven that drinking large doses of alcohol over a long period of time damages numerous tissues and organs including the brain, heart, skin, stomach and intestines, pancreas, liver, muscles, eyes, and arteries throughout the body.

In treating a person with alcoholism (the disease), it is not surprising to discover that the initial trigger to drinking was depression. In fact, a major national study concluded that if a person has both mental-emotional problems and problems with alcohol or other drug abuse, the odds are that the mental-emotional problems came first. And the most common psychiatric symptom is, of course, depression.

The depressed person is at increased risk of trying other self-medicating street drugs besides alcohol. These matters are discussed in this book; for now it is enough to say that research is continuing to clarify the special relationships between particular emotional symptoms and particular street drugs. For example, anxious people may choose alcohol, heroin, or another sedating drug precisely because it sedates the anxiety problem.

This brings us to an important observation about psychiatric-emotional problems like depression and anxiety, and alcohol and other drug use: the past fifteen years has seen an explosion of clinical knowl-edge and research findings that help us understand the intertwined and intersecting relationships between mental health problems and alcohol and other drug abuse. In fact, my own studies in this area, now called "dual disorders," began a little earlier, in 1978. In that year I first reported my observation that many of the mental and emotional relapses of young people were due to undiagnosed and untreated alco-hol and other drug abuse.

A final, personal note: People who are severely depressed—especially if they are suffering from an anxious-agitated depression or from a depression that causes them to move and speak slowly—are easily identified as depressed by others. But these people are in the minority. Most depressed individuals look, act, and speak in a perfectly normal manner, and thus can hide their depression from others, even their loved ones. Here is an example.

Some years ago I convened a group of clinically depressed people in my office to begin a support group. Eight women eyed each other in my waiting room. Then I invited them into my office and we all sat down. I broke the heavy silence by asking if anyone could describe how she felt in the waiting room. One brave woman bit her lip, looked at me to avoid the faces of the others, and then spoke:

> *I felt like running out of the waiting room because I could see that I didn't belong in the group. I was sitting there feeling so down I felt like crying—hopeless, sorry for myself. In contrast, I could see that the rest of you are calm, composed, and in control. I just knew I didn't belong in a group with the rest of you. I'm deeply depressed and Dr. Pepper said that everyone in the group would be depressed like me. But you all are obviously fine.*

The other seven women proceeded to say pretty much the same thing, each in her own words.

The point is this: If you are depressed, you are not alone.

—BERT PEPPER, M.D.

Acknowledgments

Special thanks to . . .

People who have lived with depression who graciously shared their stories with me in hopes of helping others.

Dr. Bert Pepper for his expert consultation about medications.

Editors Tim McIndoo and Cathy Broberg for so carefully reading many drafts.

Friends who provided encouragement and humor along the way.

Introduction

Sometimes it comes out of the blue, with seemingly no reason at all. Other times it follows a tragic event, a difficult childhood, or a setback in life. It can come slowly or suddenly. However it comes, depression takes away confidence, joy, and, sometimes, the will to live.

People sometimes deny depression. In their struggle to keep going, they may tell themselves, *I have a lot to be grateful for,* or *Other people seem to bounce back from hard times, so I should be able to too,* or *Maybe if I just worked my self-help program harder, I'd feel better.* They may also feel ashamed to have depression. But depression is not a person's fault, and willpower alone will not make it go away. Depression is a disease with a life of its own.

If you have started to recognize some signs of depression in yourself, you probably have a lot of questions. *Is it really depression? Who can I talk to about these things? Where can I find help? What's the use anyway?*

By reading *I Can See Tomorrow,* you can begin to get some answers to these questions. As with any serious problem, understanding what's wrong and getting better is not strictly a do-it-yourself project. The purpose of this book is to provide a sound starting point for your journey. It's written to help you understand depression and to give you reason to hope.

When you're depressed it's hard to read and absorb a lot of information. You may find your mind wandering. It may be hard to concentrate. That's okay; if it's important, you'll come back to it. This book is written so that you can dip into it as needed. Most of the chapters include these five main sections:

- Basic information, along with what is known from research or clinical experience. (The appendix offers additional details.)
- *What if I am in recovery from addiction?* This section is written to address the special concerns of people who are recovering from addiction to alcohol or other drugs.
- *What does this mean for me?* This part will help you apply the information to your own situation.
- *Further questions.* Here you will find commonly asked questions and answers about the chapter's topic.
- *What can I do to help myself?* At the end of each chapter, you will find suggested activities and ideas to think about. You may choose to do some or all of the suggested activities right away or you can come back to them anytime.

Is This Me?

As you read the following examples of how four people struggled with depression, think about yourself. Then read the short statements that summarize the concerns illustrated in each person's story. Do you have similar concerns? If so, put a check mark in the space next to the summary statement. This isn't an exercise to diagnose yourself; it's just to get you started thinking about your own feelings and experiences, and how they compare to the feelings and experiences of other people.

Cindi has always been quiet and sensitive. Her feelings are easily hurt and she is quick to doubt herself. She takes life seriously: when others laugh, she only smiles. She can't remember ever really having fun. For Cindi, life is something to be endured. Recently she read a newspaper article about someone who was being treated for depression, and now she wonders if she might be depressed too.

"I've never really been happy. Could I be depressed? Others who are being treated for depression don't seem so different from me."

Michael has always been skeptical of counseling and believed that people who went into therapy were weak or just wasting their time. While he has had his share of troubles, he has always handled them by himself. Now he's not so sure he can do that anymore. He feels as though a black cloud is hanging over everything. Nothing is going right and he's cutting himself off from friends. For weeks his world has been growing steadily bleaker.

"I thought I could always snap out of feeling blue by myself. But I can't seem to shake this sense of gloom."

Everyone who knows Kendra knows her quiet, sure sense of herself. Life seems to always go smoothly for her. Two years ago, however, Kendra's partner in life died. This triggered lots of unresolved grief from previous losses to resurface. When all this grief first hit, she accepted it, knowing deep down that it was time to walk through it. But now, after two years, Kendra feels worn out. Life seems pointless and she has no energy left to handle all the usual daily problems.

"I've been through many hard times, but now I am experiencing a deep loss (a loved one, health, job). I can't seem to get back on track."

As a young man, Ty was talented and his future looked bright. But now in his middle years he looks back on his life and thinks, *I haven't accomplished anything. I'm stuck in a job that doesn't mean anything to me. Other people have happy families and I don't.* Ty feels more and more hopeless and is planning ways to end his life.

"I feel hopeless and sometimes have thoughts of suicide."

As these stories illustrate, depression can come in many forms. Whatever form it takes, depression is a very real disease. But as you will see in the following pages, depression can be understood and treated. Overcoming depression—or learning to live a life with it—is no easy journey. Yet recovery from depression is possible. In this book you will read the stories of people who have recovered from depression. Learning how they have lived with depression and the choices they have made can open the door to your recovery.

CHAPTER 1

What Is Depression?

Depression is more than feeling blue. It is a condition that involves the body, mind, spirit, and all the connections in between. It is often biological, affecting things like appetite, sleep, and energy level. Depression is psychological, affecting how you feel about yourself. It also affects your social life, making you want to withdraw from people.

WHAT ARE THE TYPES OF DEPRESSION?

The intensity of depression varies. Milder depression is called *dysthymia*. People with dysthymia can usually continue working, carrying on their daily tasks. But they have a harder time doing so than most people and don't enjoy what they are doing. Major depression or a *major depressive episode* is more severe. It usually prevents people from going to work every day and seriously interferes with daily functioning in other ways.

How can you tell if you are depressed? If you were to go to a therapist for an evaluation for depression, the therapist would ask you a series of questions to learn more about you, just as a physician would ask questions and conduct tests to learn whether you had diabetes or heart disease. Depression, as any other illness, has a set of distinct symptoms.[1]

Major Depression

Here's a list of symptoms of major depression. If a person has a major depression, some of these symptoms will have been present for at

5

least two weeks. Before you continue reading, think of how you have been feeling on most days during the past two weeks. Then use this list to start thinking about your situation. Give this exercise some time and thought. Don't try to force a yes if a symptom doesn't really describe your experience. You might want to ask a trusted, observant friend or family member to help you evaluate yourself, especially if you feel unsure that you are having a certain symptom. Place a check mark (✔) in front of each symptom you have experienced in the past two weeks.

Cornerstone Symptoms

In the diagnosis of major depression, one or both of the following symptoms are present for at least two weeks:

- *Depressed mood.* I feel sad and down almost all day.
- *Apathy.* I'm not interested in doing the things that used to give me joy or pleasure. When I try to make myself do these things, I lose interest.

Other Symptoms

Staying within the time frame of the last two weeks, which of the following symptoms apply to you?

- *Significant loss of appetite nearly every day.* Nothing tastes good to me. I'm not trying to lose weight, but I've lost quite a bit in a relatively short period of time anyway. I'm just not interested in eating.
- *Significant increase in appetite nearly every day.* It seems as if I'm eating all the time. But I don't feel full for long so I'm soon eating again. Or else I eat even when I'm not hungry. I just keep stuffing myself with food.
- *Sleeping too much almost every day.* I'm sleeping much more than usual. I'm always so tired, but I'm not sick. It just feels good to go to bed early and have the day over with. I sleep as late as I can in the morning or nap during the day. Sometimes I wonder if I am sleeping to escape from all my troubles.
- *Having trouble sleeping almost every day.* Often I lie awake for a long time when I go to bed at night. Or if I fall asleep easily, I

wake up during the night for no apparent reason and have trouble going back to sleep. Sometimes I get up at four or five in the morning just because I know I'll never get back to sleep again. This sleep problem doesn't make sense to me. There's no one making noise when I'm trying to sleep, I'm not drinking too much cola or coffee, and I haven't changed my schedule in any significant way.

- *Slow personal tempo.* I feel as if I'm going in slow motion. When I start projects that usually take a short time, I find sometimes that I am not done hours later. I don't know what's happened to the time and why I can't seem to get moving. My friends have noticed that I am moving much more slowly than usual.
- *Fast personal tempo.* I have difficulty sitting still. I jiggle my foot when I'm sitting and move from activity to activity without completing anything. I feel agitated. My friends tell me this is different from my usual pace.
- *Fatigue.* I feel exhausted nearly every day. I don't have the energy I used to have to get things done. I feel worn out, tired. Everything is just too much, and getting anything done requires tremendous effort. I can't find any reason for it. I'm not sick that I know of, and I don't have any new demands in life.
- *Feelings of worthlessness or extreme guilt almost every day.* I don't just feel bad when I make a mistake; I feel horrible, as though I'm worthless. I feel like a burden to others. Sometimes the feelings of worthlessness are so strong that I think maybe I don't even deserve to exist. When I read my journal, I see I am writing mostly negative things about myself.
- *A lot of trouble concentrating almost every day.* I have trouble reading a simple magazine article or following the plot of a television show. When I read, I have to start the page over and over again and still I wonder what I just read. When I try to watch a program, I lose my concentration. I have trouble deciding on simple things, such as what to order at a restaurant. When I meditate, I have trouble letting my mind clear and focus. In the past, I have been able to concentrate.

- *Recurrent thoughts of death or suicide.* I often think it would be better if I were dead. Sometimes I think about ways I could kill myself and even plan ways to do it. Sometimes I don't really put myself into what's going on around me because I think I might be dead soon anyway. I think about how others might react if I were to kill myself.

Find out whether the symptoms you checked match those of major depression. Place a check mark (✔) next to each item in this list that applies to you.

- One of the cornerstone symptoms is present.
- At least four of the other symptoms are present.
- These symptoms have been present for at least two weeks.
- They are present nearly every day.
- They represent a significant change from the way I usually feel.
- They are not due to another problem, such as a medical illness or the effects of drugs, including drug withdrawal.

If you checked all of the above statements, it is likely that you are experiencing a major depressive episode. Someone who has an episode of major depression experiences at least one of the cornerstone symptoms of low mood or apathy, plus several of the other symptoms described in the preceding section. Often it is a fairly distinct episode, with a beginning and an end. It may last months or longer.

If you checked off several but not all of the statements, you may be experiencing a less intense type of depression. People experience depression in many ways.

Dysthymia

Some people find their symptoms do not fit the criteria for major depression, but they recognize that they are not happy and have not been happy for a very long time. They may be experiencing a different type of depression called *dysthymia*.[2] Dysthymia is similar to major depression, but differs in the following ways.

- It is characterized by low mood and at least two of the other symptoms of major depression. In other words, not as many symptoms of depression are present.
- It lasts for a long time, at least two years and sometimes more. In fact, a person may not be able to remember a stretch of time longer than a couple of months when he or she felt free of symptoms and content with life.
- It usually doesn't have a distinct beginning and end. A person may be so accustomed to it that it seems normal.

It used to be thought that dysthymia was simply ingrained in people's personalities—that they were just born unhappy, pessimistic, and withdrawn. In the early 1980s this view began to change, and the field of psychiatry classified dysthymia as affective, or mood disorders. This signaled a change in prognosis: the change occurred because psychiatry began to recognize that people with dysthymia *could* change; they *could* get better.

Double Depression

Some people who have dysthymia may also experience a major depressive episode. When this happens they sink even lower than they have become accustomed to. This is referred to as *double depression.* Treatment for the major depression can help these people get back to where they can function again, but they may still feel the low mood and other problems associated with dysthymia. From there they will need to continue working to learn how to live with or reduce their symptoms of dysthymia.

Bipolar Disorder

Depression can be part of a mood disorder called *bipolar* or *manic-depressive illness.* In this illness, people experience both mania and depression. They may have normal periods in between. Although unusual, some people with bipolar disorder have repeated manic episodes with no depression.

Usually it's the manic phase that alerts other people to the fact that something is wrong. During a manic phase, people feel euphoric or as if they are high. Just as people who are depressed feel overly pessimistic, people in a manic phase feel overly optimistic. Their self-esteem is inflated and they may become grandiose. For example, they may believe that their ideas will save the world or alter the course of history. Their personal tempo greatly increases; they talk almost nonstop, are easily distractible, and need very little sleep. They may quickly become irritable if they are challenged or crossed. During the depression phase, the person gets no pleasure out of activities; in the manic phase, the person dives into them excessively, sometimes with harmful consequences. During a manic phase, people do things such as suddenly deciding to fly to a faraway place with little or no thought of the daily responsibilities they leave behind; they may spend all their money on shopping sprees or poorly thought-out investments.

Seasonal Affective Disorder

One form of depression comes and goes with the seasons. Some people notice that they become particularly depressed during the winter months. (For some people this is reversed. The depression occurs in the summer months.) This type of depression, which is gaining more attention by mental health professionals, is called *seasonal affective disorder*, or SAD.[3] (*Affective* in this context means "emotional.") SAD has some distinct features, including

- Decreased level of energy, initiative, or creativity
- Increased eating, especially sweets and starches
- Weight gain
- Increased sleeping, including naps during the day
- Avoidance of friends; decreased socialization

OTHER WAYS TO LOOK AT DEPRESSION

Endogenous Depression

Looking at the way depression arrives—whether it arrives for no apparent reason or in response to an unhappy event—can help you understand it better.[4]

When depression seems to come for no reason, you might wonder what is happening to you. You might feel confused, even alarmed. *Everything was going okay . . . and then out of the blue, I could tell I was getting depressed.* Depression that seems to have no immediate cause is sometimes called *endogenous depression; endogenous* means "birth within." The depression seems to come from within us, not from something that happens to us from the outside.

Mia's story illustrates this kind of depression. She had had periods of sadness during her life, but they had always subsided on their own within a couple of weeks. Then one time she found herself experiencing a more serious depression, lasting well into two months.

> *I felt suicidal but had no reason I could pinpoint. . . . I had many things in my past that would justify being depressed—violent relationships and so on—but I had made lots of changes in my lifestyle and worked on my issues. Then one day I just called the emergency room at the local hospital and told them something was wrong but I didn't know what. They told me to come in for a psychiatric evaluation.*

If you've experienced endogenous depression, you may be frightened because it seemed to come for no reason. Once free of it, you may worry that it will come again without warning. However, keep in mind that if depression does come again, you may be more familiar with the subtle symptoms leading up to it and be able to get help sooner. In addition, as you become more familiar with depression, you may discover things about your lifestyle that contribute to depression or do not help protect you from depression. For example, you may not have realized how difficult your job or marriage (or any other situation) was until you were well beyond your first depression. Or, you may have begun to recognize grief or losses in your life that are still affecting you today. Even if you never do find the reasons for your depression, you can still get effective treatment and move beyond it.

Reactive Depression

If you know why or when your depression seemed to begin, it is most likely a *reactive depression*. This means that the depression occurred in reaction to something that happened to you. Ellen recalled the beginning of her depression, when she was in a very difficult situation:

> *I hated the man I worked for and I had a very unhealthy relationship with him. We antagonized each other frequently. He was verbally abusive—and I was paralyzed with fear of losing my job.*

Gabe also knew when his depression began:

> *When my wife came home and said she wanted a divorce, the bottom just dropped out.*

Even if your sadness seems to begin with a specific event in your life, it can turn into a depression that takes on a life of its own. It may begin as the blues, a setback, a grief reaction, and everyone (including the sufferer) thinks, *This too shall pass.* Often it does. But when it does not, it evolves into a major depression. People with a reactive depression often blame themselves, thinking, *Other people lose their jobs or get divorced but they get on with their lives. How come I can't just shake off my sad feelings?* What they don't realize is that they have crossed the thin line between a reaction to a tough situation and a major depression. Willpower and reminders to cheer up will not be effective.

The terms *endogenous* and *reactive* might help us understand different ways depression can appear. But depression doesn't always fit neatly into these categories. Many people carry the seeds of depression within them and the depression only "comes out" with a tragedy or a difficult time in life.

There are three other ways depression can be recognized: Activity level, overcompensation, and isolation.

COMMON THREADS OF DEPRESSION

Activity Level

Depression may express itself in different activity levels. With a *retarded depression*, people eat more, sleep more, and generally move more slowly. *Retarded* here means slowed or reduced in speed. With an *agitated depression*, people find that they eat less, sleep less, and have trouble sitting still. They are restless and their minds are racing and crowded with thoughts. People with *atypical depression* experience two symptoms of retarded depression: They sleep more and eat more than usual. They also experience another painful symptom: an oversensitivity to rejection. Their feelings are very easily hurt.[5] Still, people with atypical depression are able to enjoy life for the most part.

Overcompensation

Many people try to overcompensate for the feelings of depression, warding it off by keeping busy. Kaylene tried to bury herself in food, activity, or sleep.

> *During the time I was experiencing the depressive episodes, I functioned well. I got involved in lots of community activities—a neighborhood recycling project, a fund drive for the preschool. I was busy raising my son, caring for my home, and working. I even began attending law school.*

Isolation

Isolation is also a hallmark of depression. People often begin to avoid friends, skipping meetings or get-togethers they once looked forward to. When friends ask them what's wrong, they are likely to brush them away with superficial comments. Some people use wit or humor to keep others away, even when they are feeling isolated. They often feel intensely ambivalent, wanting to be alone on the one hand but feeling very lonely and unwanted on the other.

WHAT IF I AM RECOVERING FROM ADDICTION?

Depression is especially complex when it appears with alcoholism and other addictions. It is probably impossible to go through alcoholism or addiction without experiencing a tremendous amount of sadness at some point. When an alcoholic or addict feels depressed, many questions arise: Is it really depression? Am I really alcoholic or am I just drinking to medicate my depression? Do I just feel low because I'm not high on cocaine anymore? Maybe I'm just not working my Twelve Step program well enough. Can I take an antidepressant medication and still be in recovery? Who can I trust to answer these questions?

It's important to know that depression and addiction can be separate disorders, even if they occur at the same time. In fact, many people experience these two disorders simultaneously. Yet many people do not get the help they need. If you are in recovery and are experiencing a major depression, it's not just a matter of working your program harder—or of giving up on the Twelve Steps altogether. Depression is another problem and requires separate treatment.

However, diagnosis and treatment of depression are complicated by addiction. When addicts drink or use drugs, they might feel very unhappy. They might even seek help for their unhappiness. But that help is unlikely to be effective. It's almost impossible to accurately diagnose a depression for people who are active addicts, even if they are honest about their use. Treatment for depression, whether it is medications or counseling or both, is likely to have little impact unless the person becomes abstinent.

Even when a person is abstinent and has started along the path of recovery for addiction, diagnosis and treatment of depression can be tricky. Many addicts in early recovery are still reeling from the effects of their addiction. Their lives may be in shambles. Families are confused and alienated, good jobs are lost, and financial and legal consequences are crashing in. On top of this lies the stigma and shame some people feel about coming to terms with their addiction. *Of course I'm depressed! Who wouldn't be?*

Later in recovery, people often struggle with the more subtle repercussions of addiction. They may feel intense sadness. *Now I can see how much of my life has been spent on my addiction. I have years that I need to make up for! And the novelty of recovery has worn off; I'm exhausted and disillusioned.* They may also be learning to deal squarely with the adversities of life without a chemical cushion—and understandably feeling the pain.

Is This Me?

Here are some stories of people in addiction recovery who also experience depression. Each story is followed by a short statement that summarizes the person's concerns. Do you have similar concerns? If so, put a check mark (✔) in the space next to the summary statement. This isn't an exercise to diagnose yourself; it's just to start you thinking about your own feelings and experiences, and how they compare to the feelings of other people who have experienced both addiction and depression.

Getting into addiction recovery was like coming home for Ben. It felt comfortable and natural. He worked hard applying the Steps to his daily life and was a mainstay at his Alcoholics Anonymous group. Now, out of the blue, he is depressed. In the past, he'd coached many others along who were struggling—he knew how to help them. But now, nothing was working for him.

"I've been in recovery for some time and it's been solid. I've been productive and happy. I'm the type of person who usually enjoys life and people. But suddenly the program doesn't seem to be working for me. I still go through the motions (usually), but I'm getting worried. I don't understand what's happening to me. Is it that the program isn't working anymore?"

Cara was beginning to realize that she has been depressed since she was a little girl. As an adolescent, her depression came out as rebelliousness and sullenness. She was alienated from others and escaped into drugs. Now, twenty years later, she is drug and alcohol free, and her life is settling down. She has continued to attend Alcoholics Anonymous meetings. However, she still feels down a lot of the time. She credits Alcoholics Anonymous and therapy for keeping her alive, but she wonders why she's still feeling depressed.

"I remember being depressed long before I started having a problem with alcohol and other drugs. In fact, I think I used alcohol and other drugs to medicate my sadness and painful feelings. I'm in recovery now. But I wonder, was my problem really addiction or was it depression? I still feel depressed."

Levi finally agreed to accept help with his drinking. No one would listen to him anyway when he tried to tell them, "I drink because I'm depressed. If you had my life, you'd drink too." Now he realizes he was being defensive and denying his drinking problem. His life was not a happy one, with or without alcohol.

"I'm new to recovery and I think I'm depressed. I'm working on my alcohol problem, but I don't think my depression is getting better."

How Is Depression Related to Addiction?

Depression complicates addiction and addiction complicates depression. People who are struggling with both often wonder, *Is it really two disorders or does it just seem like it?* Many people do have two disorders—both addiction and depression—but other people experience a depression that is directly related to their addiction.

Some people claim that they used alcohol or other drugs because they were depressed, or conversely, that they became depressed because of their addiction. These aren't just excuses; they may be picking up on a subtle pattern.[6] Research on the relationship between alcoholism and depression has found that for most alcoholic men, the alcoholism comes first and the depression develops later. For most alcoholic women who are depressed, the opposite is true; the depression develops first, then the alcoholism.[7] But regardless of the order, people who are addicted will need treatment for that; overcoming depression, in itself, will not cure addiction. In the same way, overcoming addiction will not necessarily cure depression; people in addiction recovery who are also depressed will often need treatment for the depression too. And since most people have a hard enough time accepting one disorder, having to come to grips with two disorders can seem especially unfair.

People who experience their first episode of depression before they develop an addiction have what is known as *primary depression*. In this case *primary* doesn't mean "most important"; it means "first" or "on its own." If a person is experiencing a clear primary depression, it's more likely the depression will need its own treatment. In fact, if left untreated, depression can contribute to relapses and difficulties in getting a strong foothold in recovery from addiction.

Mary's story is an example of primary depression. She remembers being unhappy and dissatisfied as a child for no apparent reason. By adolescence she was experiencing friction with her parents and had started drinking and taking drugs. (Depression often appears as rebellion during adolescence.) As the years went on, she continued to drink and use drugs, and attempted suicide numerous times. Finally she received treatment for chemical dependency, got into stable recovery, surrounded herself with loving people, and found a job she liked.

> *My recovery from addiction was amazing to me. I felt better quickly, and my life became better. I was active in Alcoholics Anonymous. I attended daily meetings, I was active in service, I found and developed a relationship with a sponsor, and I sponsored other people. I was able to complete a bachelor's degree, get married, and have a child. I practiced the Twelve Steps and discovered a spirituality I had always sought and, like the Big Book says, my entire attitude and outlook on life changed. On the surface, things looked great. But I wasn't sure much had changed on the emotional level. I still experienced random deep depressions that came without any apparent trigger.*

Depression is also called primary if it begins when a person has been abstinent from alcohol and other drugs for a period of time, at least six months. (Remember that primary means that the depression occurs on its own and not as a direct consequence of addiction.) This is what happened to Larry three years into his recovery:

> *I began to doubt the power of the program and the changes I'd made because of it. I don't know just how the gray curtain came down on me, but it seemed that as hard as I was working with my recovery from alcoholism, I should be much more "joyous and free" and experiencing the "freedom from bondage" that I kept witnessing in the program. I didn't feel this way at all. I felt cynical, lonely, and hopeless. I even thought of killing myself—that's not like me at all.*

Larry was doing everything right, but he knew something was missing. He had the experience of being in a solid program of recovery from addiction, doing well for a long time, and then experiencing depression. In his case the depression seemed unrelated to his alcohol addiction.

If the depression occurs after a person has started using or drinking, it's called a *secondary depression*. *Secondary* doesn't mean "of secondary importance"; it means "it occurred second," or that it is related to the alcohol or drug use. Secondary depression might stem from the growing feelings of futility in trying to control alcohol or drug use, or from facing the pain of all the mounting consequences of addiction. Most people with secondary depression find that their feelings of depression subside in just a few weeks as they stay abstinent and start a new life. In other words, as abstinence grows stronger, the depression lessens. Darrell wasn't depressed before he started drinking. He had had the normal ups and downs that everyone has, but he was always able to shake them off. This was different: Darrell experienced a secondary depression.

> *When I went into treatment, I was devastated. I thought my problem with alcohol was my own business. Now everyone knew it. I felt ashamed and guilty. I felt like I let everyone down, most of all myself.*

Looking back, Darrell realized that when he started depending on alcohol, his world got smaller, and he began to lose his happiness. Staff at the treatment center talked to Darrell about his depression and suggested that he allow himself more time in recovery before deciding whether to pursue treatment for depression. The staff told him his depression might resolve itself with abstinence and a solid recovery program. Darrell did experience fewer and fewer symptoms of depression as he progressed in his recovery from addiction.

Most people have trouble objectively untangling their own stories of depression and addiction. It's especially important for people in early addiction recovery to find a professional to talk to about their depression. Getting a good assessment can help make recovery from depression possible.

And remember that the picture is not entirely bleak. People who are recovering from addiction may have special advantages in dealing with depression. They have already overcome adversity in dealing with their addiction and have developed strengths because of that. There are other stories throughout this book that show how people in recovery from addiction have found help for their depression.

WHAT DOES THIS MEAN FOR ME?

Some people think depression is synonymous with feeling blue. After a bad day at work or an argument with a friend they might moan, *I'm so depressed!* What they really mean is that they are sad, unhappy, discouraged, or frustrated. This casual use of the word *depression* is unfortunate because it can trivialize the state of true depression. Depression is a serious disorder. Every year thirty thousand people in the United States kill themselves,[8] and for most, untreated depression is the reason. There is hope for people with depression, but first, they need to know that it's not something they can just snap out of.

The difference between feeling down and being depressed is like the difference between having too much to drink one night and being an alcoholic. Someone who is not an alcoholic and drinks too much one night can wake up the next morning and say, *Whoa! I overdid it last night. I'm not going to do that again!* And, not being an alcoholic, that will probably be the end of further problems with alcohol. But everyone knows what happens when alcoholics say that. Maybe they will be able to quit drinking for a while or carefully control their intake. But if they are alcoholic, just deciding not to drink too much will not solve the problem. In time, they'll have another drinking episode. It is not their fault or necessarily something they want. But until they understand that they are an alcoholic, and what that really means, they will remain stuck in the same cycle.

It's the same with people who are simply feeling blue. Someone who is not truly depressed but is in a low spot can say, *Hey! I'm getting gloomy. I'd better lighten up here! I think I'll go out and do something fun and try not to let my troubles get to me.* People who are not clinically depressed can probably do just that. But for those experiencing a major depression, the best they may be able to do is act or bury their symptoms in busyness. Over time, the depressive symptoms will reappear, and the person will become even more self-blaming and discouraged.

As with the people who don't recognize their own alcoholism, these people will remain stuck until they understand they have depression.

Chapter 1 has looked at different types of depression, a long list of symptoms, and a variety of ways that depression presents itself. In later chapters, we'll be looking at the ways depression affects not only feelings, but the body and mind as well.

FURTHER QUESTIONS

I don't exactly fit the description of depression. Does this mean I should just try to forget about it?

No, not at all. Your feelings and situation are just as serious as anyone's and need just as much attention. If you are experiencing any of the symptoms described in this chapter, it means that something is going on inside you. You may want to get a thorough assessment by a professional. And even if you are not diagnosed as having a major depression, it's still important to take care of yourself and continue to explore the path you are on. Emotional pain is difficult, no matter what the label is.

Does it matter what kind of depression I have?

Knowing the variations of depression can help you see that you are not alone. There are different types of depression and not everyone fits a mold. Some people think, *I'm not feeling like so-and-so did when she was diagnosed with depression, so I must not really be depressed. Whatever I am experiencing must be something different.* Two people can be depressed but have different symptoms.

Learning about all the ways that depression can express itself can also give you more ideas about how to help yourself. There are many things you can try on your own. Some ideas may come from reading this book.

If your depression doesn't begin to clear even as you make changes in your life and try new things, you might need help from a professional. This does not mean your efforts have failed. Rather, a thorough assessment by a skilled, experienced, mental health professional—one who has seen hundreds of people with varying degrees of depression, during all phases of the illness—can give you more information to work with. Professionals have a perspective that can help you see yourself in ways that you cannot see on your own.

WHAT CAN I DO TO HELP MYSELF?

When you're feeling depressed, you may start to wonder, *Where can I even begin?* Here are some first small steps you can take to help yourself.

1. Have you completed the exercise in this chapter (pages 6–8) to assess your symptoms of depression? If not, this might be a good time to do so.
2. If you're concerned about your symptoms of depression, who can you talk to? If you have friends or family members who would understand and be good listeners, this might be the time to talk to them. Showing them the checklist you filled out can be a good starting point of discussion.
3. Do you feel you need a professional assessment to learn more about yourself and your feelings? Could you call a mental health center to make an appointment? The information in chapter 4 can give you more guidance in how to find what you need.
4. Maybe you are already seeing a therapist for other issues. Have you talked about your symptoms of depression with him or her? Now that you understand what they are, and have names for them, perhaps you'll feel more able to do so.
5. Listen to other people talk about themselves. Do you know some people who say they are struggling with depression? In the past, perhaps you haven't noticed that a friend or acquaintance was acting depressed. Perhaps you haven't paid full attention to them. But now you know more about what they may be experiencing. Could you ask them about their depression? Listening to them can (a) help validate their experience; (b) help you learn more about depression; and (c) perhaps help you get a clearer picture of what is going on inside you.

For people in addiction recovery: Is there a mental health professional in your community who understands both chemical dependency and depression? You might need to ask around in the recovering community to get some names.

CHAPTER 2

Who Has Depression?

YOU ARE NOT ALONE
If you're depressed, you might feel alone and think that nobody could understand the depth of your pain. You might be embarrassed or ashamed about your feelings and think that others would look down on you if they knew how you felt. The fact is, you have company: Art Buchwald, Dick Cavett, John Cheever, Kathy Cronkite, Abraham Lincoln, Theodore Roosevelt, Mark Rothko, Suzanne Sommers, Rod Steiger, and William Styron are a few of the well-known people who have experienced depression.[1] Many of them have spoken or written about their depression so that their stories might give strength and hope to others.

Depression is so prevalent that it has been called the "common cold" of mental illness. Over eleven million people in the United States experience depression every year. Estimates vary widely, but a recent study, published in the *Archives of General Psychiatry*, found that 17 percent of adults experience a major depressive episode at least once in their lives. Another 6 percent have experienced, or will experience, dysthymia (the type of low-level, chronic depression that usually starts when a person is young). About 2 percent of the general population have or will experience a bipolar disorder (the type of depressive disorder that varies from one extreme to the other—being manic during some periods of time and very depressed at other times, or having episodes of mania without depression). Looking at all types of depression, a large number of the population of the United States—about one-fifth of all adults—can expect to experience some type of depression in their lifetime.[2]

While both men and women are vulnerable to depression, the rates are higher among women. About twice as many women as men experience a major depressive episode (as well as dysthymia) in their lifetime. Surprisingly, though, the rates of manic depressive illness among men and women are about equal.[3] Women with small children have among the highest rates of depression.[4]

There is also more depression among people at the lowest income levels.[5] People living in poverty may be somewhat more vulnerable to depression because they may become discouraged and disheartened by their situation and then develop clinical depression. It may also be that people at higher income levels become less able to function when they get depressed and, therefore, lose their jobs and move into lower income levels.

Even though depression is more common among some populations, it can and does strike people in all walks of life.

People of Any Ethnic Background Can Become Depressed

Although people of all colors and races can become depressed, rates of depression are generally found to be somewhat higher among Latinos than whites. Overall, blacks have lower rates, but one large national survey found that the highest lifetime rate of depression was among black females between the ages of thirty-five and forty-four years.[6]

People of All Different Educational Backgrounds Can Become Depressed

People who have an advanced college degree are just as likely to become depressed as those who have not graduated from high school.

People of Any Age Can Become Depressed

Some studies show that the likelihood of becoming depressed is higher among younger people, and wanes a bit with older age.[7] But it's a myth that young people are in the best years of their lives because "they have everything to look forward to" or that older people should be immune to depression because they are in their "golden years" and past the demands of career and growing families. Each age has its own challenges.

People in Solid, Loving Marriages and Those Who Are Alone Can Both Become Depressed

Some studies do show that in general, the rate of depression is highest among the unattached—those who are separated, divorced, widowed, or never married.[8] But this is not a simple cause-and-effect situation. Depression prevents some people from entering into intimate relationships or destroys the relationships they have built. For others, the loneliness of being single sets the stage for depression. Regardless, both attached and single people are vulnerable to depression.

People in All Sorts of Careers Can Become Depressed

Having a stable, prestigious, or well-paying job doesn't protect a person from depression. And all types of companies are increasingly recognizing that many of their employees are depressed. Companies care about this for humanitarian reasons, but they also know that depression among employees affects the bottom line.

(Depression is a major national expense. It costs $44 billion every year in the United States. Businesses lose $23.8 billion annually due to absenteeism and decreased productivity caused by depression. Another $12.4 billion is spent in treatment costs, and $7.5 billion is lost as a result of suicides that are caused by depression.[9])

WHAT IF I AM RECOVERING FROM ADDICTION?

People with addiction are much more likely to experience depression in their lifetimes than people without addiction. While the numbers vary greatly, many research studies find that the rate of depression among alcoholics is about two to three times higher than in the general population. And for those who have been dependent on both alcohol and other drugs, the likelihood of depression is even higher—about 10 percent higher.[10] Manic-depressive illness has an especially high correlation with addiction. Over half of the people with a manic depressive illness have a drug or alcohol problem.

WHAT DOES THIS MEAN FOR ME?

In short, depression can happen to anyone. And it happens to tens of thousands of people every year. It happens to people with high incomes and to people with low incomes, to men and to women, to people of all races, to young and to old. Being depressed is not a sign of moral weakness, lack of intelligence, or incompetence. If you experience depression, it is not your fault and it is not something to be ashamed of.

FURTHER QUESTIONS

Why do the statistics about who has depression matter to me?

Just this: they mean you are not alone. This is not your own private hell. What you are experiencing is something that others have experienced too. And many of them have not only survived, but also have come out the other side. Because so many people have experienced depression, employers and society in general are recognizing it. Depression is losing its stigma. More and more, people understand that it is not a matter of "cheering up" and "counting your blessings." More people understand that depression strikes people from all walks of life: ambitious and successful people; sensitive and giving people; rich and poor; high and low IQ; tough and soft. If you are experiencing any type of depression, you do not need to be ashamed or apologetic.

I hear and read more about depression now than I did in the past. Is depression increasing or are people just talking about it more?

Depression has always been a significant problem, but it is becoming more visible because people are acknowledging it. It is losing its stigma as more and more people see that it can be treated. Most people with a depressive disorder can find a treatment method that works. It is tragic that anyone would suffer alone and without help when so much is known about how to treat depression.

WHAT CAN I DO TO HELP MYSELF?

Even though depression is widely recognized today as an illness that can strike anyone, many people still feel some shame about it. Do you feel shame about experiencing depression? Perhaps it would help if you could *really* give yourself permission to believe that anyone could experience depression. To help yourself understand this fact on a personal level, try the following action steps.

1. Have you thought you were the only one with depression? Imagine a room full of one hundred people. In your mind, count off twenty of them: these people have known depression too. (*For people in addiction recovery:* Imagine walking into a large, open Alcoholics Anonymous meeting of one hundred people. In your mind, count off thirty of them: these people have experienced depression similar to yours. Let yourself sit with this for a while.) If you fully take this in, you may find yourself able to be more compassionate with yourself and others. Even though the world can look like it is filled with busy, happy, productive human beings, you are not alone in your suffering.

2. Some people who are doing very well in life now have experienced depression in the past. You might not know it to look at them. Whom could you interview to find out if they have experienced depression? A friend? A family member? Someone in a recovery support group? Could you ask the question of your whole recovery group? This exercise may bring you a surprise. You may find that a very active and lively person has experienced depression in the past. As you do the exercise, remember that you do not have to talk about your own experience if you don't want to.

CHAPTER 3

What Causes Depression?

Depression is a mystery. Some people can live most of their lives free from depression and then get caught in its grip. Other people battle it their whole lives. Still others go through life without ever experiencing depression. This illness has probably existed since the beginning of time, it has been heavily researched, and still we do not know its cause.

Most likely, depression is many disorders, not just one. Consider the term *fever*. At one time, it was thought that fever was an illness unto itself. Today it's known that fevers are caused by many different illnesses and conditions. Some fevers are caused by chicken pox, some by pneumonia, and some fevers are due to blood poisoning from a cut. Having a fever is a sign that something is wrong.

Similarly, depression is a sign that something is wrong—physically, spiritually, or emotionally. And regardless of how the depression gets started, our whole being is affected. Current theories stress the biological and chemical nature of depression, and that is where we will begin.

BIOLOGICAL FACTORS

Genes

If you are experiencing depression, you might be able to look back at your family—grandparents, parents, siblings—and see that you're not the first one in your family to experience it. Depression often runs in families. In fact, some families have a rate of depression that is two to three times higher than the rate in the general population.[1] This is true for all types of depression, but especially for bipolar disorder, the type of depression that is characterized by extreme swings between depression and mania. A person who has bipolar disorder probably has relatives with the disorder and other forms of depression. Because of these strong patterns, one theory is that depression is carried in the genes, in the chemical makeup passed down to us from our parents.

But just because depression runs in families does not necessarily mean it is genetic. It could mean that the family environment creates a climate ripe for depression. For example, when parents are depressed, they probably cannot convey to their children the love and warmth they would if they weren't depressed. In turn, the children may become more vulnerable to depression. Or the children may subtly take on the negative beliefs of a depressed parent. So how can we know whether a disorder like depression is caused by genes or by the mood of the family?

Researchers do special studies of families to test out these theories. Family studies can get quite complicated because there are so many factors involved. But let's take a short detour to understand how these special studies are done.

One of the most fascinating types of studies is twin studies. Twins are either identical or fraternal. If they are identical, they share all their genes. If they are fraternal, they share about half of their genes, just like any two siblings. In either case, they usually grow up in the same family. If depression is carried in genes, identical twins should always be exactly concordant for depression. This means that if one twin is depressed, the other one should be, too, because they have exactly the same genetic makeup. On the other hand, if depression is caused by the environment—by the way a person is raised or the mood in the family—the rates of depression in identical twins and fraternal twins should be pretty similar.

Are identical twins equally depressed? No. But there's enough similarity in their rates to give researchers hope that they are on the right track. Studies vary quite a bit; depending on the study, the concordance rate for identical twins ranges from 33 to 70 percent.[2] In other words, at least one-third of the time, if one identical twin is depressed, the other identical twin will be too. The rate is even higher for mania; if one identical twin has experienced a manic episode, there is an 80 percent chance that the other identical twin has too. You might think, *Well that's only natural, twins are so emotionally and physically close to each other.* That's where comparisons come in. Fraternal twins' concordance rate for depression is only 20 percent. This rate is a bit higher than the general population rate, but far less than that of identical twins. If depression was caused just by the environment—the way the family operates—fraternal twins should have the same rates of depression. But they don't. Therefore, it's likely that something in the genes is making a difference.

Another way to research how genes affect depression is to compare adopted children and biological children.[3] If depression is primarily genetic, then the biological children of depressed parents should have a higher rate of depression than other people, regardless of how healthy their home life is. Researchers studied a group of depressed adults who were all adopted at a very young age. They interviewed and examined records of these people's biological parents and adoptive parents. The researchers found that the adoptive parents, the parents they grew up with, had a rate of depression that was about the same as for the general population—about 12 percent were depressed. But when the researchers went back to the biological parents, they found almost three times more depression. The suicide rate among their biological relatives was even higher. In their depression, the group of depressed, adopted adults were more like their biological parents than their adoptive parents. This suggests that their genes influenced their depression. (These researchers also studied adopted people whose biological parents were *not* depressed. They didn't find higher rates of depression in this group. Being adopted, in itself, doesn't seem to make a person more prone to depression.)

If depression is genetic, what exactly might the genes be carrying? Genes carry small bundles of information. It is unlikely that they can carry the whole story of depression. Instead, they might carry information about resiliency to stress, perception of rejection, sensitivity to emotional pain, or ability to experience joy and pleasure. Many of these states can be regulated or affected by brain chemicals. So genetic makeup may lay down the biological structures that alter brain chemistry and make people more or less vulnerable to the characteristics that add up to depression.

Genetic studies of depression show that people carry something in their genes that may make a difference in whether or not they develop depression. This is especially true for bipolar disorder. It might be that different forms of depression have different genetic strength. Just as important, genetic studies show that something besides genetic makeup contributes to the tendency to become depressed. If depression were passed down the generations as clearly as eye color or body build, identical twins would have exactly the same depression experiences. It is clear from twin studies that this is just not true. Something else is also contributing to depression.

Brain Chemistry

The most popular theory of depression is that some people who are depressed have imbalances of important chemicals in the brain, called neurotransmitters. Neurotransmitters carry messages between the nerve cells in the brain. They begin in one cell, go out into an open space between the cells (a *synapse*), and then move into another cell. During this journey through the brain, neurotransmitters carry important signals about the need for food and sleep and people's basic mood states. In depression, these messages break down. Brain cells on both sides of the synapse are oversensitive or insensitive, which in turn create a deficiency of a particular kind of neurotransmitter. In depression, the two types of neurotransmitters that are thought to be most affected are serotonin and norepinephrine.

At this time, there is no way to measure levels of neurotransmitters. Because the levels of neurotransmitters can't be measured as they flow through the brain, some inferences have to be made. For example, it is known that medications that affect neurotransmitters also affect depression. So if antidepressants improve depression, and they also affect the level of neurotransmitters, it's likely that neurotransmitters play an important role in depression. In fact, as we shall see in later sections, researchers developing new medications to treat depression focus on medications that increase levels of serotonin or norepinephrine.

Someday, the theories about brain chemistry will be far more complete. There are many theories about the brain and how it works, but very little proof. Nothing in the brain holds still long enough to study it; chemicals and electrical impulses swarm throughout it. And the brain is so well protected that it can only be studied indirectly. Although the chemical balance theory is the most popular theory of depression today, it's important to remember that it is only a theory, not a hard and fast explanation. Future studies will produce a clearer understanding of the brain and of depression.

Biological Cycles

One of the most important rhythms of the body is its daily sleep schedule. Interruptions in this schedule may influence depression. While we might not go to sleep at the same time every night or wake up at the same time every morning, what happens while we are sleeping is intended to be finely tuned and regular. Every night, we drift in and out of five different sleep cycles. Any changes in the pattern of these cycles—whether we are conscious of them or not—can affect how we feel during the day. Researchers and sleep clinicians can observe sleep cycle patterns by hooking a person up to an electroencephalogram monitor (EEG). Researchers have found that when people are depressed, their sleep cycles are disrupted.[4] Typically, they spend less time in the stages of deep sleep and more time in REM or dream-time sleep. (REM stands for Rapid Eye Movement; our eyes dart back and forth under our eyelids while we dream.) People who are depressed seem to enter REM sleep much faster than normal when they fall asleep.

It's commonly thought that depression causes sleep problems. But some theorists say the opposite may be true: a dysregulation of the sleep-wake cycle may be the root of the depressive disorder. It is true that sleep is critical to well-being, and any changes in it can have far-reaching effects. Some treatments for depression are based on this theory. The Japanese have developed a type of therapy called *Morita therapy* in which extensive sleep is prescribed for people who are extremely depressed.[5] Other methods of sleep therapy for depression recommend the opposite—decreasing the amount of sleep.

So far we have looked at how the physical processes in the human body may cause depression or are affected by depression. But as pointed out by the studies of identical twins, something besides physiological processes contributes to depression. Environment—the circumstances in which people grow up and in which they live as adults—also influences depression.

ENVIRONMENTAL FACTORS

Painful Childhoods

The events and experiences of childhood can contribute to depression. Children are very impressionable, and the ideas they get about the world and the people in it stay with them for a very long time. Psychoanalytic theory says that it is our earliest relationships—those with our mothers and fathers—that teach us how to think about the world, what to expect of others, how to feel about ourselves, and how to react to events. In other words, the beliefs we form when we are very young can influence all our future relationships.

For instance, at a very young age we form our beliefs about whether or not we can trust others, and trust is the foundation upon which our future relationships are built. It is also in the earliest years that we form beliefs about whether or not we are worthwhile and lovable. We are all born utterly dependent. Growing up is a process of learning to be independent, to be separate from that all-important first caretaker and yet to form dependent, intimate relationships. Ideally, children learn during this long process that they can be separate individuals—be the people they really are inside—and be loved by someone else at the same time. If for some reason they learn the opposite—that their needs won't be met, that they can't be who they are and still be loved—they may

34

decide that they don't deserve to be loved, that they are defective. When people don't know how to love themselves or form loving connections with others, the stage can be set for depression.

How does it happen that people form these negative beliefs about themselves and others? It can happen when children are neglected, ignored, or hurt. It can happen if a parent physically leaves a child through death or divorce, or emotionally through addiction, depression, or other disorders. But even people in the healthiest of relationships can be hurt and can develop negative beliefs. Nobody is to blame for this. While insensitive or cruel parents can and do hurt children both physically and emotionally, no parent is perfectly tuned in to a child's needs at all times, and some hurts are inevitable. No human being, on either side of the relationship—adult or child—can perfectly balance the needs for dependence and independence.

Regardless of what causes a difficulty, problems people have in their earliest relationships tend to recur later in life. The early beliefs people form about themselves and others can become lifelong patterns: the belief that others cannot be trusted, that others will always leave, and that they themselves are unlovable or defective. As people struggle to establish connections with others, these patterns and beliefs go before them and wreak havoc, leaving them vulnerable to isolation, loneliness, and low self-esteem—all ingredients for depression.

The following section looks at two environmental factors that can result in depression: losses and learned helplessness.

Losses

If people suffer extreme losses, they may develop depression. Any loss can produce grief and pain, but losing a loved one is one of the most painful things human beings have to bear. Being in relationships has been critical for survival and the continuation of the human species, but loss is inevitable and uncontrollable. People can do everything right and others will still leave, whether by choice or by death. Other types of loss can also adversely affect people. Loss of anything that sustains them—a hobby, a pet, a job, or the ability to do certain activities as they grow older—can trigger a grief reaction. Over time, as people continue to suffer more loss—parents, family members, close friends, homes, jobs—the stage may be set for depression. Ultimately, loss can result in loneliness. Many people who are depressed feel very lonely, even if they have other people around them.

Why do some people who experience losses become depressed while others don't? As noted earlier in this chapter, some people are biologically more vulnerable to depression. Some people have had particularly difficult experiences with intimacy when they were young children, so they started on shaky ground. Others may have a solid foundation, but experience such painful or repeated losses that they cannot find their way out of grief. And because grief from the past accumulates, the loneliness they are feeling may be deeper than what might be reflected at the moment.

Learned Helplessness

As we grow up, ideally, we learn that we are competent individuals who are capable of taking on and succeeding at new tasks. We learn and believe that we are capable of giving and receiving love, and that we matter to other people. But some people learn just the opposite. They learn that no matter what they do, it is not good enough. Numerous experiences lead them to believe that they are deficient—that in spite of every effort, they will not succeed, obtain love or a feeling of self-worth. They begin to feel helpless and hopeless. This, too, can set the stage for depression.

In studies, researchers have found that animals lose the will to live and grow if they are repeatedly hurt and can do nothing about it. For example, in one study, rats were placed in a pool, and no matter how hard they swam, they couldn't swim out. On other days, they were placed on a pad that delivered electric shocks. What happened to these animals? Over time, they stopped doing anything in these situations. In the pool, they didn't swim; in the cage, they just stood on the electric pad. This is called *learned helplessness*. It also might be called giving up. It is sad to think about these animals in research experiments.

It is tragic that this very same phenomenon occurs to human beings every day—not in scientific experiments, but in real life.

It's not hard to understand how learned helplessness can happen to prisoners of war and victims of war-torn countries like Bosnia and Herzegovina, or Rwanda. People in these situations have little control over what happens to them. But the same phenomenon can occur in relatively peaceful times in stable countries. Can you think of situations in which your behavior has no effect on what happens to you? Imagine yourself in a job where no matter what you do, your boss and co-workers are critical and negative. Or in a marriage where your spouse hits you even if you've prepared the perfect meal. Or in a family, as a child, where whatever you do to get noticed is met with disregard. Pretty soon, you might give up. This is learned helplessness.

If people are in a hurtful situation and nothing they do will improve or change it, eventually they may begin to believe they are defective human beings. Unconsciously, they may begin judging *themselves* instead of the situation they are in. Instead of thinking, *This is an impossible relationship*, they begin telling themselves, *I am no good*. Even when new opportunities come along—the possibility of a new job, a new friend, a chance to begin again—it may be too late. Their helplessness has become hopelessness, and they don't try anymore. They remain stuck in their isolation and their feeling of worthlessness, both of which are ingredients of depression.

In the above sections, we've looked at theories about how depression might be caused by biological makeup or environment. But indirect causes are possible too. Sometimes depression may be caused by, or made worse by, another issue.

ASSOCIATED FACTORS

Sometimes depressive symptoms are part of another problem such as nicotine addiction or hormonal changes. In these situations, treating the main problem may help take care of the depression. Or simply understanding the relationship might help you tolerate the depression better while the main problem is being treated.

Hormonal Fluctuations

Hormones are intricately connected with neurotransmitters—the chemicals that carry messages between the nerve cells in the brain. Hormones are messengers, too, carrying information about the growth and development of all the body's systems. Changes in our hormonal levels can create changes in our brain's neurotransmitters—and consequently our mood.[6] In fact, we know that some hormonal diseases, like hypothyroidism, can cause depressive symptoms.

Many women can trace their mood swings to changes in their hormonal levels. Women's monthly menstrual cycles follow a delicate interchange among several hormones, but especially estrogen and progesterone. Anything that changes the balance in the hormones can influence depression. As a result, many women have special concerns about depression.

I'm on birth control pills.

Birth control pills can trigger or intensify depression in some women. For women who are prone to depression, this can be a special risk factor and a reason to consider another form of birth control.[7]

I just had a baby. I'm happy about it, but I don't feel the joy and excitement that I thought I would.

It is relatively normal to have the "baby blues" for about three to seven days after giving birth. But if this feeling continues, it may develop into what is known as *postpartum depression*.[8] This depression may be partly due to the stresses of having a newborn at home and all the responsibilities and changes that go along with it. But most likely, the changes in hormonal levels that occur during and after pregnancy alter the neurotransmitters and, as a result, mood.

If you have a history of depression, you may be at higher risk for postpartum depression. Some women are ashamed to be depressed after they've had a baby, because they believe they should be happy. They're reluctant to tell people how they really feel. Postpartum depression is real, and it happens to a certain proportion of new mothers. Being depressed does not mean you are an unworthy parent! But it does mean that you need—and deserve—to get help as soon as possible so that you and your baby can get started on a healthy track.

My depression is worse during the days before my period.

We've all heard jokes about PMS (premenstrual syndrome), so it's easy to come to the conclusion that PMS isn't a very serious problem. But some women are severely affected by the physical and emotional changes that occur during the week before menses.

PMS has been also called *premenstrual dysphoric disorder* and is now part of the most recent *Diagnostic and Statistical Manual* (1994), an important resource for mental health professionals.[9] The criteria for premenstrual dysphoric disorder are similar to the symptoms of depression:

- Feelings of depression, hopelessness, or low self-worth
- Anxiety, tension, and edginess
- Tearfulness and oversensitivity to criticism or rejection
- Irritability and anger
- Decreased interest in things that usually give joy or pleasure
- Difficulty concentrating
- Fatigue, sleeping a great deal
- Overeating and craving certain foods (especially starches)
- Feeling overwhelmed or out of control
- Physical symptoms such as bloating, breast tenderness, joint pain, headaches, or weight gain

Women who have a history of depression may be especially vulnerable to premenstrual dysphoric disorder.

Some women are not attuned to their bodies and may not recognize the relationship between their mood states and natural cycles. This is unfortunate, because there is a solution for most of these situations. A gynecologist can do a thorough assessment and suggest ideas that may involve regulating a woman's hormone system. Time and patience are needed in making the adjustment, but it can greatly improve a person's life.

Other women are relieved just to know the pattern exists. They can tolerate the feelings of depression because they know their source and they know the feelings will pass in a few days. For instance, LaVonda struggled with depression through most of her life. She recognized that she had a particularly difficult time during the days before her period, but she learned to identify those times and ride them out. For many women, just knowing where they are in their menstrual phase can offer great reassurance; what they're reacting to may very well be real, but the intensity of their response may be magnified by the shift in hormones.

I'm middle-aged but not in menopause yet, and my moods are really changing.

Symptoms of depression can be related to hormonal changes in midlife. Years before menstrual periods actually stop, subtle symptoms may appear. This phase is called the *peri-menopausal phase*, or *around the menopause*. Many women may be prepared for mood swings with actual menopause, but most are not even thinking about the changes in hormonal levels that begin years before this. As a result, the mood swings of peri-menopause surprise them. Some of the same symptoms that occur during PMS can occur during peri-menopause.

I'm in menopause and I know my depression is at least partly related to that.

Not all women experience depression during menopause. But for some, depressive symptoms can be severe. A woman who is concerned about depression during menopause may want to consider estrogen replacement therapy. Estrogen is often recommended during menopause to protect women against bone loss and heart disease. There are pros and cons to using estrogen replacement; one benefit is that it may decrease the depression associated with menopause. The best course of action is to see a gynecologist familiar with a wide range of options for treating depression during menopause.

Nicotine

Many people who are depressed find it much harder to quit smoking than people who are not depressed.[10] Smokers may not even recognize that they are depressed because nicotine acts as a stimulant or upper. In this way, smoking can be a form of self-medication. The nicotine may produce two effects: (1) it may change low mood by affecting the brain's neurotransmitters, and (2) it can act as a stimulant, giving an energy boost. As long as people continue to smoke, they can hold many depressed feelings at bay. Whether smokers have major depression or more subtle feelings of low mood, hopelessness, and anxiety, they may not recognize that they are depressed. Then, of course, they cannot recognize that their depression is making it hard for them to stop smoking.

When people who are depressed try to quit smoking, they may feel a tremendous amount of emotional pain and sadness. This is more than the sense of grief about not having cigarettes. It is more than the irritability and craving that most smokers feel during withdrawal. For some, it is the reemergence of depression that has been mostly hidden or at least controlled. The depression may be so intense that they decide they would rather smoke—with all its dangers and consequences—than experience the depression. Because women have a higher rate of depression, they are especially prone to being depressed cigarette smokers.

Cara experienced this kind of problem. She was forty-five years old, successful at work, in a loving relationship, and was the type of person people enjoyed being around.

> *I've always been a real joker and liked to make people laugh. That's how others see me. But when I try to quit smoking, it's a whole new ball game. I hate to even try quitting when I'm working full time because I know I'll just sit at my desk and cry. I don't know what happens to me. Everyone else is amazed too. And worried. I know I need to quit smoking, but I'm scared to even try. I get so depressed I can barely work.*

Does this mean that cigarette smokers who are depressed are simply doomed to continued smoking? Not at all. Research suggests that people can cope if they get vigorous therapy for depression during the withdrawal period. Some very promising research has been done using cognitive-behavioral therapy—a therapy that teaches people strategies to endure and lessen negative mood states—for smokers who are depressed and trying to quit smoking. Surprisingly, there is no research on the use of antidepressants for people who are depressed and are trying to quit smoking.

In one study, conducted at the Department of Psychiatry at the University of California in San Francisco, smokers who were depressed were given two forms of treatment. One group received cognitive-behavioral therapy and the other received simple encouragement and support. Six months after treatment, half of the smokers who had received cognitive-behavioral treatment were still not smoking. In comparison, only 12 percent of the group who had just received support and encouragement were not smoking. The researchers speculate that the cognitive-behavioral treatment might have helped the smokers deal with both their depression and their nicotine withdrawal symptoms.[11]

There is growing acceptance in the United States that the pleasures of smoking are not worth the health risks. As a result, many people have quit smoking and using tobacco products.

More people are also becoming aware that cigarette smoking may be a sign of depression. An article in the *Journal of Family Practice*, for example, recommends that physicians (a) view smoking as a sign that a patient may have an underlying depressive disorder and (b) assess and treat the depression.[12] Now that the link between cancer, other serious health problems, and nicotine is understood, it's clear that using nicotine to control depression is not a good option.

If you are a smoker who's having trouble quitting, you might have an underlying depression. If so, it's especially important for you to get help with that illness. Both psychotherapy and antidepressants may be useful. But whatever kinds of help you choose, it's important that you know you may experience at least some symptoms of depression while you are going through nicotine withdrawal. These symptoms may include crying or feelings of hopelessness. But this doesn't mean you are spiraling into a full depression. As you learn ways to cope with your depression, you'll be able to maintain your new nicotine-free life.

Physical, Sexual, and Emotional Abuse

The emotional impact of abuse is often severe and long lasting. The abuse may have been physical, sexual, or emotional; it may have been huge or seemingly small; it may have occurred during childhood or the adult years. But the memories of abuse are often painful. Some people try to deny the emotional impact, thinking the abuse was minor or that it occurred so long ago. But denial does not lessen the pain. Many people who have experienced abuse are swept with feelings of despair, shame, and hopelessness even years after the abuse.

Some abuse survivors may have a pattern of feelings and experiences that fit another diagnostic category, called *post-traumatic stress disorder*. Or they may experience both post-traumatic stress disorder and major depression. Either way, the feelings that abuse survivors experience are real. But good therapy can help survivors begin to find their way out of the shadow of abuse.

Abuse is an especially important topic for many people who are recovering from addiction—the incidence of sexual abuse appears to be much higher in this group.[13] Uncovering memories of abuse can trigger a relapse. If you are recovering from addiction and have experienced abuse, it's important to get help for the feelings that abuse causes.

Alcoholic Homes

Children of alcoholics are not automatically depressed. In fact, most research studies find that the majority of children of alcoholics do not experience major depression or any other disorders.[14] But if you are involved in a self-help group such as Adult Children of Alcoholics (ACA), you may object. You may think, *I see how alcoholism or addiction has affected children! Every week in my group, many people talk about their depression, and many are in therapy or on antidepressants. How can you say that being an adult child of an alcoholic and being depressed are not related?* When you attend groups such as ACA, you may see many adult children of alcoholics who are depressed because going to these groups is one of the ways they are seeking help for their depression. Therefore, their numbers may be "overrepresented" in Adult Children of Alcoholics groups.

Possible Environmental Contributions to Depression in Alcoholic Homes

Still, there is no doubt that in some alcoholic families, the environment can be ripe for developing depression. First, the alcoholic parent and child may not be able to bond with each other because the alcohol or other drug use is in the way. If the parents are continually high, they may not be able to pay attention to the child in the careful and consistent way that promotes bonding.

Second, the child may be forced to trade roles with the adult, disrupting the process of gaining independence. The child may end up taking care of the alcoholic's needs. For instance, the child makes suppers or gets the little children off to school because Mom or Dad is too impaired. Sometimes taking care of parents' needs is more subtle. It can mean that the child is working far too hard to excel at school or sports so that Mom or Dad won't be disappointed and get drunk. These are not supportive, happy situations for a child.

Third, there may be abuse in alcoholic homes. The family may be split apart. The growing children can feel despair at having no impact on what is happening around them. Or, perhaps worse, they may mistakenly believe that they are the cause of all the turmoil. Children who absorb these beliefs about themselves will struggle in future relationships and may be prone to depression.

Possible Biological Contributions to Depression in Alcoholic Homes

In some cases, biology contributes to depression in children of addicts. The children may inherit a genetic predisposition toward depression. In some families, alcoholism, anxiety, and depression seem to occur together. Sylvia notes

> On my mother's side of the family there's a lot of depression and alcoholism. My mother was depressed and so were her sisters and her mother. My two brothers and my dad were alcoholic. My dad was also depressed—in fact, he killed himself.

This type of pattern has led theorists to speculate whether there is something called the *depression spectrum disease*. They hypothesize that whatever is being genetically transmitted shows up mostly as depression in women and as alcoholism in men. The National Institute of Mental Health funded a large study of depression to test this theory. They found that alcoholic women often had both depression and alcoholism in their family. They also found that the alcoholism in their family, particularly among the women family members, was often a by-product of a primary depression. But this wasn't so for alcoholic men; their alcoholism seemed to run more true—their relatives are more likely to be alcoholic than depressed.[15]

Some studies show little connection between depression and addiction in generations of families, and there is no definitive research on the subject. Still, the question remains, *Is there a genetic link between depression and addiction, and if so, what is it?* It may be that some people inherit a special sensitivity to alcohol or drugs. It may also be that they inherit a deficiency in serotonin, one of the natural chemicals in the brain that seems to play an important role in depression. Another possibility is that some people inherit serotonin levels that change significantly in the presence of alcohol. It may also be that there are two types of connections between depression and addiction: genetic and environmental. For some people, the connection may be largely genetic. Their family history is filled with examples of both depression and alcoholism, and indeed, some people have both disorders. In other families there is very little overlap between depression and alcoholism.

Eating Disorders

Depression often develops along with eating disorders, particularly bulimia. People with bulimia go on eating binges; some may vomit afterwards. For most people, the eating disorder occurs first and the depression follows. Shame, low self-worth, and feelings of hopelessness often develop as the eating disorder takes hold. These feelings are part of depression too.

Medications for Blood Pressure and Other Physical Problems

Medications for various physical disorders can cause or contribute to depression. When depression is inadvertently caused by medication, it is called *iatrogenic depression*. For example, some medications used to treat high blood pressure produce fatigue and low mood in some people.[16] If you think this is happening to you, talk to your physician. But never just stop taking your medications! Medications change the body's chemical balance, and changing it suddenly may be dangerous. Physicians can usually find other medications that can treat the physical problem without causing depression.

Sometimes older people who are on multiple medications experience depression. Family members, friends, and sometimes even doctors may assume it's just a normal grief reaction that comes with age and loss. But in some cases the medications themselves—or the interactions among them—may actually be the culprit. Again, talking to a physician is very important.

Seasonal Changes

Seasonal affective disorder (SAD) occurs primarily in northern latitudes, during the winter months when the days are shorter.[17] Therefore, the strongest theory is that SAD is caused by a lack of light. We need a certain amount of light each day to regulate our hormones, especially one called melatonin. Since hormones are intricately connected with the balance of neurotransmitters in the brain, a change in these critical hormones can produce unwanted changes in the level of neurotransmitters.

Serotonin, too, may play a role in seasonal affective disorder. Some research suggests that serotonin levels naturally fall during the winter months and that some foods, such as carbohydrates, increase serotonin levels. These ideas fit in quite well with symptoms of SAD: People with SAD usually feel worse in the winter and crave carbohydrates.

Alcohol and Other Drugs

The chemicals we put in our bodies affect our natural chemical balance, which is designed to keep our moods stable. Here's an overview of the effects of various substances on our moods and state of mind.[18]

Alcohol

Alcohol is a depressant. It slows or depresses the body's general level of activity.

Sleeping Pills and Anxiety-Reducers

Barbiturates and tranquilizers, such as Xanax and Halcyion, are also depressants. A person taking them may feel sedated. For people who are already depressed or who have a tendency toward depression, these types of drugs may bring the depression—and possibly suicidal thinking—to the surface.

Marijuana

Long-term marijuana use can cause *amotivational syndrome*. In this state, people don't care about participating in life or doing much of anything. The effects of long-term marijuana use can resemble depression.

Opiates

Opiates are painkillers. Withdrawal from opiates can include feelings of anxiety, fear, and dread. Even normal events in life can seem extraordinarily painful if you are used to medicating pain and then stop doing so.

Cocaine and Other Stimulants

One of the hallmarks of cocaine withdrawal is depression, which may last several days or even weeks. This is thought to be a rebound effect—the depression is a reaction to the euphoria that the use of cocaine or other stimulants creates.

Gender

While the basic causes of depression may be the same for everyone, women may be more vulnerable to depression than men are. The rate of depression among women is about twice as high as it is for men.[19] Clinicians often note that relationships are especially important to women, and they may be more prone to depression when relationships are disrupted.[20] Women may also be more apt to evaluate themselves negatively, resulting in low self-esteem. In society, women often face more responsibility for families, more financial difficulties, discrimination, loss of opportunity, and domestic violence, all of which can contribute to depression.

WHAT IF I AM RECOVERING FROM ADDICTION?

Using Chemicals

People in addiction recovery often have used chemicals that can create or magnify depressive symptoms. It isn't known whether the effects are short term or long lasting. Some theorists believe that long-term exposure to drugs creates changes in the brain that may take weeks, months, or even years to reverse. This of course is particularly true for people who have used a lot of drugs for a long time. Some of these changes in the brain may leave a person an addict. In other words, the body remembers the disease, and the disease begins again if drug use is resumed. But it is also possible that the changes produced alter the body's response to pleasure and reward. These changes may leave people more vulnerable to depression—and even more so if they were already vulnerable to depression for some other reason.

Using Nicotine

Alcoholics and other addicts have much higher rates of smoking than the general population. This is one of the great ironies for people in addiction recovery. They avoid the tragedy of dying from alcohol or other drug use, only to die of nicotine use.

Some alcoholics and addicts do not want to quit smoking because they are afraid the stress of quitting might trigger a relapse to their alcohol or other drug use. However, research doesn't bear out this fear. A research study looking at people who quit alcohol or other drugs and nicotine at the same time found that their relapse rates to alcohol or drugs were about the same as for people who kept smoking.[21] In other words, quitting smoking did not set them up for relapse.

If you are in addiction recovery and are depressed, you may be especially afraid to quit smoking. As you read earlier in this chapter, nicotine can hold depressed feelings at bay. However, you can get help for depression. Then, when you have a more stable emotional foundation, you'll be more able to stop using tobacco. As a bonus, your self-esteem—knowing you've beaten the nicotine addiction—will probably be higher.

What Does This Mean for Me?

If you are depressed, it may be hard to put your finger on the exact cause. Depression is a complicated phenomenon, and people are such delicate, finely tuned animals that the exact causes of depression may never be known. But you can be assured that rarely do people "bring it on themselves."

For most people, there won't be one simple cause; usually several events must conspire to create this painful disorder. To complicate matters further, a factor that causes depression in one case may actually be a result of depression in another case. For example, an imbalance of neurotransmitters may cause a person to become isolated, which in turn can lead to depression. In this case, the chemical imbalance in the brain would be the cause of depression and the isolation would be the result. On the other hand, forced helplessness or isolation can cause changes in brain chemistry. In this case, the apparent imbalance in brain chemistry would be the result of the isolation rather than the cause.

Exploring the possible causes of depression can give some sense of control to a person who feels helpless and overwhelmed. But whether or not people understand the causes of their depression, treatment can usually help them cope with, or recover from, depression.

Further Questions

I struggle with depression. People say that depression is hereditary; does this mean my children will become depressed too?

No, not necessarily. Even though there does seem to be a genetic role in the development of depression—especially bipolar disorder—most children of depressed people do not become depressed. Creating a healthy environment to grow up in can help decrease any child's chances of growing up with depression. However, we do not yet know what part of depression is due to genetics and what part is due to the world and events around us. Therefore we cannot predict who will become depressed.

My parents were alcoholics when I grew up, and now I am an adult experiencing depression. Is being depressed part of being an adult child of an alcoholic?

Being an adult child of an alcoholic can mean many things. Some parents do not develop alcoholism until late in their life, so its impact on their children may be relatively small. Or, the parent who is not addicted may be able to take over the family in a way that minimizes the effect of the other parent's illness. Or, biologically, the genetic load for addiction and other problems is not transmitted. In other words, there is no automatic relationship between being a child of an alcoholic and being depressed. In fact, most research studies find that the majority of children of alcoholics do not experience major depression or any other psychiatric disorders.[22]

Isn't depression simply a chemical imbalance?

At this point in time, depression as a chemical imbalance is an important theory but not accepted fact. Because the brain is so mysterious and unavailable to study, the chemical reactions in it cannot actually be seen or measured. But it is a good theory for several reasons: (1) It fits with what is known about treatment of depression. For example, antidepressants seem to work by changing the levels of important brain chemicals. (2) It gives good ideas about more biochemical treatment methods to explore. (3) It helps take away the stigma that so many people feel about being depressed. The chemical balance theory has one important shortcoming: Some people with depression only take antidepressants and yet see improvements; they do not work on their own or with a therapist to understand the nature of their depression and what they can change in their life to improve it. Although this works for some people, most people with depression need more than a strictly biological approach.

WHAT CAN I DO TO HELP MYSELF?

It may seem as if depression comes from nowhere, for no reason. But this isn't true; depression comes from somewhere, even if you can't easily identify the reason. Once you begin to understand what may cause or at least worsen your depression, you may see ways to overcome, lessen, or prevent it.

1. This chapter has described many possible causes of depression. Look over all the factors listed below. Do you think any of these may have caused your depression? Put a check mark (✔) next to the items that apply to you.

- *There is a history of depression in my family.* Think back to your parents and their brothers and sisters. Has anyone had depression? What about your grandparents? Are there any patterns of depression going back several generations? You may not find depression per se. Depression was not always officially diagnosed in earlier generations because so little was known about it then. To discover whether there is a history of depression in your family, you may have to think of how these people would be viewed nowadays. If you are adopted, do you know anything about the mental health of your biological relatives?

- *I had a particularly painful childhood.* How stable was your home life growing up? Did you form a warm and welcoming bond with at least one parent? Did the adults in your life meet your physical and emotional needs? If you aren't sure what your childhood was like, you might be able to find out from other relatives.

- *I have experienced significant losses in my life.* Think back to important people or things that you no longer have in your life. These might include friends and family members, pets, and even activities or abilities. When did these losses occur? Did you have the time and support to cope with them?

- *I use negative self-talk.* Spend a day noticing how you talk to yourself. What thoughts do you have in your own mind about who you really are? Are you positive and accepting, or do you constantly put yourself down? Are there any words you automatically use to talk to yourself when you are in difficult situations? Do you blame yourself or do you coach yourself along?

- *I have experienced physical, sexual, or emotional abuse.* If you have experienced abuse, have you gotten help for it? Or have you tried to put it out of your mind and assume it has no relevance to your life now? For many people, the effects of abuse stay with them for many years.

- *I am struggling with an eating disorder.* If you have an eating disorder, have you sought help? If you are attending a self-help group or seeing a therapist, have you talked about the possibility of depression?

- *I am taking medication for high blood pressure or another physical disorder.* If you are taking any medication, could you talk to your physician about the possibility of depression being a side effect?

- My *natural hormonal cycles are affecting me.* If you are a woman, are you aware of your natural hormonal cycles and how they may be affecting you?

  - Do you experience premenstrual symptoms? Some women rate their mood every day on their calendar, using a scale from one to ten, with one being totally downhearted and ten being ecstatic. Over a period of three to six months, you should be able to a discern a pattern, if there is one.

  - Have you recently had a baby?

  - Are you in your early to mid-forties, or expecting to reach menopause within the next three to five years? If so, you may be in the peri-menopause phase and could therefore begin experiencing depressive symptoms.

  - Have you reached menopause? If so, and if you are experiencing depressive symptoms, have you discussed options with your physician?

- *I have noticed that I experience increased depression during certain seasons.* Do you sleep more, feel more tired, eat more during the winter or the summer months? Some people become depressed, or find their depression worsens, in certain seasons of the year. Most often seasonal affective disorder occurs in the winter months, but it can also occur in the summer.

- *I am taking sleeping pills or tranquilizers.* Some of their side effects include depression.

- *I am in early recovery from alcohol or drug addiction.* Some of the residual effects of drugs can cause depressive symptoms.

2. Look back over the list of possible causes of depression. Notice which ones you checked. Knowing what may be contributing to your depression can give you hope and may guide you in the steps you need to take to get better. Just as there are often reasons for depression, there are solutions. As you reflect on these thoughts, is there anyone you can talk to?

CHAPTER 4

What Can I Do About My Depression? Psychotherapy

Telling a person with depression to just cheer up is like telling a drug addict to just say no to drugs. Once a person becomes depressed, willpower has little or no effect. Depression is an illness that runs its own course. However effective treatment is more available now than ever before. And most people who recover from depression are amazed at how much better their lives became after treatment.

The two main treatments for depression are medication and psychotherapy, or a combination of both. Different people respond to different types of treatment. A psychologist, social worker, or psychiatrist can do a thorough assessment and recommend the best type of treatment for a particular individual. Some people start with psychotherapy and later add medication; others start with both psychotherapy and medication. Chapter 4 looks at psychotherapy and chapter 5 looks at medications.

WHAT IS PSYCHOTHERAPY?

Psychotherapy is talk therapy. *What good will it do to talk about my depression?* you may wonder. But psychotherapy is more than just talking about depression; it is a way to help people understand their depression—its causes, its effects, and its management. Psychotherapy can be extremely effective and often is the treatment of choice for depression. It can help break the cycle of depression. The therapist can be a companion in the darkness, helping people to see where they are and to find a way out.

The psychotherapy component of treatment is important for three reasons. First, uncovering the sources of depression can give people ideas and courage to try new ways of living. Making these changes may decrease or eliminate the depression. Second, people can learn where their vulnerabilities lie, so that they may be able to anticipate and prevent future depressive episodes. Third, it's a great relief for people to get some support and understanding from an objective person.

There are many approaches to psychotherapy, many more than we can examine in this book. We will discuss generally how psychotherapy works. Then we will take a closer look at cognitive-behavioral therapy, an approach that was designed specifically for the treatment of depression.[1]

Most of the various approaches to therapy cover some common ground. Here are some of the main topics that are typically discussed in therapy. How deeply any of these are explored depends on you and your therapist's approach.

- Assessment. At the beginning of therapy, your therapist will probably ask many specific questions to discover whether you are suffering from depression. (Many of these questions will be similar to those you asked yourself in chapter 1.) As therapy goes on, your therapist will continue to evaluate the severity and persistence of your symptoms of depression and make recommendations accordingly.
- Childhood. How happy were you as a child? Is there depression in your family? When you were growing up, how did you learn to deal with your feelings? Were there any traumatic events in your childhood that could be affecting how you feel about yourself and your world today?
- Current and past relationships. How much support have you had in your life? Are you able to establish intimate relationships? Are you lonely?

- Unresolved grief. What loss have you experienced in your life? Have you had the time and safety you've needed to resolve this grief? Is grief affecting you today?
- Stress. What everyday stressors are you experiencing in your life now? Can any of them be lessened?

Over the course of several sessions, you and your therapist will begin to see patterns in the ways you think, feel, and act in the world. Many of these patterns are healthy and sustaining, but others are self-defeating and keep depression going.

One reason people often (and inadvertently) continue negative patterns is because there is something they still need to learn. For example, people who repeatedly pick friends who are unkind may continue to do so until they realize they have a right to compassion and respect. When they can see this and believe it, they will begin to choose new friends. However, if they don't see the pattern and their part in it, they are likely to repeat it.

People also continue negative patterns of living because the behavior served them well at one time. For example, those who learned as small children not to challenge authority because they got severely punished may continue to be passive as adults, even in the most demeaning situations. As children, being passive may have meant survival. As adults, it can mean not getting important needs met. It's very difficult to immediately drop old behaviors when they become ineffective. But therapy gives people another perspective and the support needed to make changes.

Cognitive-Behavioral Therapy and the Circle of Change

Cognitive-behavioral therapy, which was designed specifically to treat depression, has undergone extensive research and refinement. In fact, some research has now shown treatment with antidepressants and treatment with cognitive-behavioral therapy to be equally effective. The studies also show that cognitive-behavioral therapy can help most people, and many therapists today incorporate aspects of it into their work.

The therapist using cognitive-behavioral therapy helps people examine their thinking and try new ways of acting in the world. This therapeutic approach focuses on how people interpret or think about the world, and how their interpretation affects what they do. The therapist is typically quite active in the sessions, almost like a teacher or partner in learning about the depression and what to do about it. People are given homework for the week and then they discuss the results with their therapist. Typically, therapy is once every week or two, and lasts for less than a year.

Cognitive-behavioral therapy is based on the idea that thoughts and feelings and behavior are intricately connected. The better people understand these connections, the better they can make changes to improve in all three areas.

Here's an everyday example: Two friends are working together in a garden in the springtime. Let's call one Mariel and the other Les. The garden is beautiful, rich with flowers of all different colors and types. A neighbor who is a community leader walks by, quickly says hello, but says nothing about the garden. Mariel thinks, *Hmmm, that neighbor must have a lot on her mind not to appreciate such a beautiful garden,* and then she feels a burst of gratitude that she has room in her heart for flowers. But Les thinks, *I guess this isn't such a great garden after all,* and he starts to feel let down. Carrying this example further, Mariel may dive into her work with renewed vigor and Les may lose interest.

This is a only a moment in two lives. But these moments become who we are. We automatically choose a response to a situation without even being aware of it. And how we respond can greatly affect our way of being in the world.

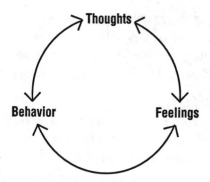

We are a delicate balance of thoughts, feelings, and behavior. When any one of these areas is affected by depression, the other areas are affected too. The purpose of cognitive-behavioral approaches is to help people see how this cycle occurs within them and what they can do to change it. Let's take a look at each part of the cycle as it occurs in depression.

How Does Thinking Affect Depression?

Our attitudes greatly influence how we perceive the events around us and our own experiences. The Talmud says, "We see the world not as it is, but as we are." In other words, we interpret the world differently depending on who we are and how we think about things. When people are experiencing depression, they tend to interpret events in a discouraging way.

Depression clouds and distorts thinking. People with depression usually view their past, present, and future negatively. In turn, the negative thoughts create more depression. It's as if everything is seen through the *opposite* of rose-colored glasses. How many of these thoughts have you had?

Negative evaluation of the past
- I haven't really accomplished anything worthwhile in my life.
- Nothing in my life has gone right.
- Every time I've trusted someone, it's been a disaster.

Negative evaluation of the present
- I'm the type of person who doesn't deserve a break.
- There's no one in my life who would understand.
- I look around me and I can see I have nothing to show for myself.

Negative evaluation of the future
- It's no use trying because nothing will ever turn out right.
- Even if something looks good, I know it won't turn out that way.
- I'm in a hole now and always will be.

If you're depressed, you probably have had many of these thoughts. And you might believe they are true. The irony is that people with depression are not thinking objectively about their situation. This is a symptom of depression, not a character flaw. People who are depressed often have trouble stepping outside themselves and seeing that their depression is causing the inaccurate view of their life. Further, their negative thoughts about themselves, their past, present, and future only serve to fuel the depression.

Sherri's story illustrates what happens with negative thinking. As her depression grew, her thoughts about herself became more and more negative:

> *I was working as an interior designer and really prided myself on having good ideas. But when I was depressed, I lost all confidence in myself. I didn't think I had anything to offer anyone. Pretty soon I started turning down projects, and when I went to meetings at the office, I didn't say much. When my boss told me they were going to have to let me go, I was expecting it; I wasn't bringing in much revenue and the company was going through hard times. I felt like a total failure. I couldn't even think about going to look for a new job.*

It's clear in Sherri's story how each part of the cycle affects the other: negative thoughts lead to withdrawal from new opportunities, which in turn lead to loss of self-esteem and feelings of sadness. Here is what it looks like in the circle diagram.

How Do Feelings Affect Depression?

You might think you're sad because you're depressed, that your depression creates your sadness. But could it be the other way around? Like the old question "Which came first, the chicken or the egg?" it's very difficult to say which came first, the depression or the sadness. This is because they are so intertwined; they fuel each other. The feelings people carry inside build on themselves.

Yes, depression does create sadness, but feelings of sadness might also play a part in maintaining the cycle of depression. To start with, the main feelings of depression are generally sadness, despair, irritability, emptiness, and inadequacy. Delise's feelings were expressed in crying. When she looked back on her depression, she remembered her feelings intensely:

> *I found myself crying frequently. I felt constantly desperate. My feelings of self-worth were gone. I seemed focused on my worthlessness. I felt suicidal.*

But many people with depression find they cannot cry and their feelings are numbed. LaVonda said:

> *By the end of that year, I felt pretty much defeated and hardly got angry at all anymore—except at work where I was angry before I even arrived. I was mostly just sad—and static.*

But even when feelings are numbed, they fuel the depression.

How do feelings affect thinking and behavior? Let's use some parts of these people's stories in the circle diagram to look at how feelings influence other parts of the cycle.

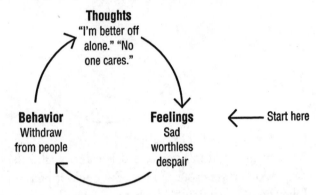

Starting at the point where the feelings occur, you can see how intense sadness can lead to withdrawal and silence, which in turn can lead to feeling more inadequate. In fact, you may have experienced this in times of depression: you feel despair and then withdraw. Family and friends try to "read your signals" and back off. If your withdrawal continues, invitations for social get-togethers stop coming. What do you think of yourself at that point? Probably less. You might believe, *I am worthless, because no one wants to be with me.* This is a tragic example of how the cycle of depression can affect a person's life.

How Do Actions and Behavior Affect Depression?

Let's take a look at the cycle from one more direction. Behavior is the third part of the cycle that is affected by, and in turn fuels, depression. When people are depressed, it's very difficult for them to behave in ways that might help them feel better. Taking advantage of new opportunities seems almost impossible.

People with depression have trouble actively participating in life. Here are the behaviors that a person with depression is likely to engage in:

- Avoiding other people
- Getting little or no exercise

- Getting stuck in a routine, not going to new places or meeting new people
- Getting stuck in minor daily chores and spending more time on them than is usually needed
- Sleeping more, or less, than usual

Taken to the extreme, any person—no matter how mentally healthy—engaged only in these behaviors would no doubt develop negative thoughts and feel unhappy.

Here's how it looks in the model we've been using:

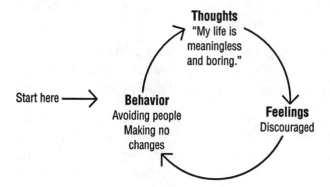

Behavior is a part of the cycle that people can change. Have you heard the slogan *Act as if and the feelings will follow*? This is excellent folk wisdom. Behavior alone can affect people's thoughts and feelings. Sometimes behavior becomes so ingrained and automatic that people have no idea of how it affects the way they view the world and themselves. For example, if every morning you allow only thirty minutes to get up and out the door to be in time for work, no doubt you will start the day feeling irritated and frazzled. Simply getting up fifteen minutes earlier and moving more slowly may create a feeling of calm that lasts throughout the day.

Putting It All Together

The balance of thoughts, feelings, and behavior is like a mobile. When one aspect of a person is affected, all parts react. It can also work like a perpetual-motion machine. As each part of the cycle reacts, it creates energy to set the next part in motion. In real life, no single aspect of a person is affected by itself. At one moment in time, a person may feel emotions, engage in behaviors, and think thoughts that keep the cycle going.

While this picture may seem bleak, there are two avenues of great hope:

- Wherever a person breaks the cycle—be it in thoughts, feelings, or behavior—the positive results "click in" and continue to transform the cycle.
- Even one small change in any part of the cycle can create an ever-growing spiral out of depression.

Let's see how this might work. To break out of the cycle of depression, it's best to work on all three parts of the cycle—thoughts, feelings, and behavior—at the same time. But for clarity, we will consider each area separately.

Changing at the Point of Thoughts

Psychotherapy is one of the best avenues to change thinking. Therapy helps people look at their assumptions, at their thoughts about themselves and their lives. When people tell someone else what their thoughts are, they may see mistakes they never recognized before. Here are other methods that help challenge depressed thinking:

- Read self-help books such as *Feeling Good*.[2]
- Use daily affirmations to reprogram automatic negative thinking and to experiment with new ways of thinking.
- Engage in daily meditation to find ways to clear the mind of thought.
- Use guided imagery to imagine a different way of being.

All of these methods can affect the way people habitually think. By allowing themselves to have new thoughts, they may find that their cycle of depression changes.

Changing at the Point of Feelings

People can do many simple things every day that have an immediate impact on their feelings. The prescribed actions may not seem logical but that's okay; feelings are rarely logical. Here are some methods to change everyday life on a feeling level:

- Avoid spending time with people when they are being negative and complaining.
- Rent comedy videos and find other ways to encourage yourself to laugh.
- Look around at your house or office or wherever you spend most of your time. Is it dull and depressing or bright and inviting? (You might need an outside opinion.)
- Get therapeutic massages.
- Read *The Woman's Comfort Book*[3] to learn ways to pamper yourself. (It has great ideas that work for men too.)

Perhaps these methods seem trite and simplistic. But there is good reason to believe that changing feelings—by changing what you see, how your skin feels, or how often you laugh—can have physiological effects.

Changing at the Point of Actions

Sometimes when people are depressed, they think, *When I'm feeling more energetic, I'll start taking walks or I'll go to the gym and work out or I'll invite my friends over for supper.* But the key out of depression is to start to change the behavior *now*—to go ahead and participate in life even when you feel you do not have the will to do so.

This is not being phony or false. Rather, it is giving yourself a chance at a "jump start" out of depression. The more new ways of being in the world that people learn, the more likely they are to find the things they need. William Glasser, a noted psychiatrist, says that we have two main needs in life: to love and be loved, and to feel worthwhile to ourselves and others.[4] If we remain isolated and uninvolved in life, there is little chance that we can meet these needs. Here are some changes in behavior that you can try now.

- Go to your usual self-help meetings even if you don't feel like it.
- Start a simple exercise program.
- Set regular hours of sleep and stick to them.
- Keep a journal.
- Paint, draw, or work with clay, and find other creative ways of expressing yourself.
- Read the book *Random Acts of Kindness*[5] to give yourself some ideas for ways to help others. Paradoxically focusing your attention on other people and acting on their behalf can make you feel better about yourself.

No single change in behavior is going to change your life. But gradually, and over time, a simple change in any one of these areas can have a ripple effect, creating changes in areas you can't predict. The key is to begin, even when you have little faith.

How Do I Find a Therapist?

With all the different approaches to therapy, and the many offices and organizations where you can go to see a therapist, you may feel overwhelmed at the thought of choosing a therapist. You may be thinking, *I don't know how to begin looking for a therapist.* Here are some ways to begin the process.

How to Find Help

As a first step, you may want to think about some practical matters. Ask yourself

- Do you prefer to see a man or a woman?
- How far you are willing to drive on a regular basis?
- How much you can afford to pay?
- Will insurance pay for your therapy?

Once you have answered these questions, you are ready to take the second step—getting names of therapists. The best way to find a therapist is by asking someone you trust for a recommendation. Do you know a friend or relative who has gotten help for depression? Could you ask your physician or clergy person for a referral? How about asking fellow members of a Twelve Step group if they have a recommendation?

Another way to look for a therapist is to call the state licensing boards of psychiatrists, psychologists, or social workers and ask for a therapist with a specialty of depression. You may also want to check with a state board to learn if there have been any complaints or restrictions placed on the therapist you are considering. (State boards often act as the Better Business Bureaus of professional practice.) Most therapists are very competent and ethical, but you may feel more secure in your choice if you check their record.

The third step is to develop a list of questions that you can use to help you decide if a certain therapist is the right person for you. After you have gathered names of several therapists, you may wish to interview them. It's important to be a smart consumer when searching for a therapist. Here are the kinds of questions you may wish to include on your list.

- How long has the therapist been in practice?
- What approach does the therapist use in treating depression?
- Is the therapist qualified to provide medications or associated with a psychiatrist who can?
- Is the therapist comfortable and experienced in working with people from a variety of backgrounds and lifestyles? This may be especially important if you have special concerns that you know will play a role in discussions about your life—for instance, if you belong to a minority group or if you are a gay man or lesbian.
- How long does the therapist typically see people for a course of therapy, and how often does the therapist generally schedule appointments?
- If the therapist is away or if an emergency comes up after hours, what arrangements are there for you to get help?

Therapists know that choosing a therapist is a big step, and most will respect your wish to collect information before making a decision. Many will give you time over the phone or in person, free of charge, to ask these kinds of questions. Be sure to take notes. And remember that there are no right or wrong answers. But in listening to two or three therapists give their answers and explanations to these questions, you will get a better feel for their approach and how comfortable you may be in working with them.

If you have a very limited selection of therapists because you live in a small community or because your insurance allows you only a few choices, it can still be useful to screen your choices. Because therapy is a very personal process, every therapist will have at least a slightly different way of doing things. Your personal reaction to the therapist is also important. As when you choose a personal physician, many therapists will have similar amounts of knowledge and expertise, but the "chemistry" between you is also important. At the same time, remember that there is no one "best" therapist. Many will be able to help you.

You do not need to choose a therapist right away and you shouldn't feel pressured by any of them. In fact, allowing yourself a few days to let the conversations settle in your mind may give you the confidence you need to proceed.

Even though it's important to be a careful consumer when choosing a therapist, you might need to choose one without a process of screening. If you are in the midst of a major depressive episode, you may not have the energy or the ability to concentrate that a screening process requires. In this case, you will need to rely more on the recommendation of someone you trust. But you can still ask your therapist some of the same questions even after you've started therapy. However you choose your therapist, step back periodically and ask yourself if you are comfortable and satisfied with the progress you are making. If not, feel free to bring it up with the therapist.

How Not to Find Help

Some people simply go to their family doctors, tell them that they are depressed, and obtain a prescription for antidepressants. They do not see anyone for psychotherapy. They return to their physician periodically, perhaps every two to three months, for a brief check on a few symptoms of depression and for a refill. Even with the best of general physicians, what's wrong with this approach?

- Without a thorough assessment, you can't be sure the problem is depression. An incorrect diagnosis can delay appropriate treatment.
- Medication might not be the answer.
- Medication alone will not help you discover and address any underlying problems that may be causing or perpetuating the depression.
- You may not get the best medication for your particular problem. Nonspecialists may not be familiar and experienced with all types of medication. They may be giving you what their clinic recommends as standard, or what they are most familiar with, rather than what may work best for you.

Unfortunately, with the growing trend in health care to provide care at a minimal level, the practice of prescribing antidepressants without thorough assessment and referral to psychotherapy is increasing. Depression is complex. It can be a lifelong, debilitating disease, and you owe it to yourself to get the most thorough treatment available.

Is Psychotherapy Working? The Patterns Of Change in Therapy

Once you have chosen a therapist and begun the work of psychotherapy, you may wonder from time to time if it is working. This is an important question and one you should pay attention to. As you assess your therapy, remember that psychotherapy can be a lot of work; it takes time and the results are not always easy to see along the way.

People experiencing dysthymia should know that this ongoing, low-level form of depression can take longer to treat than major depression. If people are predisposed to have low mood, this pattern will not change quickly or easily. Still, over time, the dysthymia can lessen. And therapy may help people live full and relatively contented lives even while they are experiencing dysthymia.

But with any depression, change doesn't happen all at once or quickly. People might go for a while without seeing any changes—and then go for a stretch where everything seems new. Sometimes people feel discouraged because they find themselves repeating old patterns that they thought were behind them. But there is some predictability to the way change occurs in therapy, and knowing this may help to keep people from feeling discouraged. It may also help people evaluate their therapy.

A group of researchers at the University of Rhode Island and the University of Houston has found a pattern to the changes people make in therapy.[6] Based on their research, they have designed a model with five phases.

Precontemplation Phase

During the precontemplation phase, people don't recognize that there is a problem or a need for change, even though others may see it. Someone in this phase may think *My boss and my wife are the source of my problems*, or *It's better to just cope with problems than to try to change them.*

Contemplation Phase

In the contemplation phase, people are aware that there is a problem, but they aren't quite ready to do something about it. At this stage a person might wonder, *Who would I go see for help?* or *Would therapy do any good?* They are starting to realize that they are depressed, that their low feelings are not just a passing mood. In this phase, a person might think, *Perhaps it would be worthwhile to work on my problems*, or *Maybe someone will be able to help me.*

Preparation Phase

People in the preparation phase are making a commitment to do something to help themselves. They might be asking others for their recommendations about a therapist, or calling local agencies or clinics. They might call a few therapists to ask them questions about how they treat depression or how much they charge. In this phase a person might think things like, *I believe I have problems and I want to work on them.*

Action Phase

When people are in the action phase, they're working hard to make changes. They are trying out new ways of thinking, new ways of acting. In general, they are taking risks that they wouldn't have taken before. This is the phase in which a person might say with deserved pride, *Anyone can talk about changing; I'm actually doing something about it.* During this phase people might keep things around as a reminder not to give in to their problems—poems or slogans for instance. They might make new friends who are supportive of their efforts. They might keep a journal, draw, or find other ways to express how they are changing.

Maintenance Phase

Some people don't recognize the importance of the maintenance phase, or even the fact that it exists. In this phase people need to continue consciously putting into practice all the changes they have made in the action stage. They might find these things happening naturally—maintaining friendships with supportive people, keeping up a program of physical activity. They're now more aware of the need to nurture themselves when they've had a hard day, instead of slipping into depressive thoughts and feelings. They recognize that old feelings and old patterns of behavior may come back and tap them on the shoulder, but they know now that they can let them go.

In reality, people don't go through these phases one by one. As they are making progress in one area of life, they might just be starting to realize a need to change another area. Or they find themselves revisiting their commitment to work on certain problems. This is all natural and part of the continuous pattern of change in therapy. The diagram on page 72 shows one way to visualize it.[7]

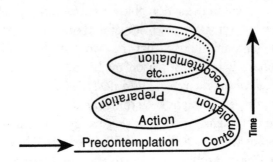

As the spiral shows, therapy is not a straight, steady line of changes. It isn't always smooth, and sometimes it feels as if it goes backward before it goes forward again. People might even wonder, *Is it really worth it?*

If depression is a signal that a person's life is out of balance and that something inside needs to be changed, therapy can help people see where the changes need to occur. Therapy gives people the time and support to make those changes. They can learn what helps them move further from depression and even learn how to prevent themselves from slipping into similar episodes in the future. Sometimes depression cannot be prevented, but therapy can help people see the warning signs and get help before they are consumed by it.

WHAT IF I AM RECOVERING FROM ADDICTION?

Depression isn't just being sad; depression also shows up in negative thinking. People who are depressed and in a Twelve Step program may notice that they are becoming cynical, doubting the power of recovery tools that worked for them in the past. They may start to skip their daily meditation and inventory, or skip the meetings they used to find helpful, thinking, *What's the use? They don't really do any good.* When they do go to meetings or see old recovering friends, they may find themselves thinking about them in negative, critical ways: *That sponsor of mine is just a bag of wind; he doesn't really know anything,* or *If*

Sally says one more time that she's grateful about something, I'm going to just walk out. They may struggle with daydreams about using or drinking as an escape. When they think about the fact that chemicals won't help, they may think about suicide. The more distorted and negative their thinking is, the more they withdraw and the more unhappy they become.

Karan looked back on her time of depression:

> *I felt guilty and didn't want to tell anyone how I felt. I felt like a phony, that all that good Alcoholics Anonymous stuff I was spouting was a lie because I was feeling so miserable. And I was ashamed. I thought I wasn't working a good enough program. I was also afraid that if I shared my feelings openly, I'd discourage a newcomer to AA.*

The more Karan mulled over these thoughts, the more sad and inadequate she felt. In the circle diagram Karan's process of thinking and feeling looks like this:

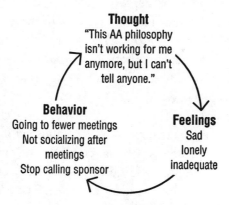

Thought
"This AA philosophy isn't working for me anymore, but I can't tell anyone."

Feelings
Sad
lonely
inadequate

Behavior
Going to fewer meetings
Not socializing after meetings
Stop calling sponsor

Karan got help, but it's easy to imagine how this cycle can lead to a relapse to chemical use.

WHAT DOES THIS MEAN FOR ME?

Depression has a tremendous impact on your thoughts, feelings, and behavior. You can feel truly handicapped in coping with the world when you are depressed. But through therapy, you can change. You may prefer one therapeutic approach over another depending on your learning style, the way you think about things, and the way you go about making changes in your life. Regardless of the approach you choose, effective treatment is possible.

FURTHER QUESTIONS
How long does therapy take?

There is no standard time frame for therapy. Most people begin to feel better within a few months, and most can see significant changes in less than a year. But according to the nature of your issues and how long you have built patterns around them, you may need more or less time.

These days, the amount of time people tend to spend in therapy is generally decreasing, and many only see a therapist for a few weeks or a few months. There is a growing trend toward a "brief therapy" model. When therapists use a brief therapy model, they take a very active role in teaching you about your depression and how to begin making changes in your life. Therapy may last only six to twelve sessions over the course of three or four months. The idea is to give you a burst of intensive help that can see you through on your own. Appointments may be built in for later dates, either as booster sessions or as a safety net to handle stressful times.

This trend toward brief therapy is due in part to the growing awareness that, for some people, much can be accomplished in a short time. It is also due in part to today's political climate—the emphasis in the United States on providing good health care at the lowest cost. Of course, brief therapy is not suitable for everyone. The amount of time you need to spend in therapy depends on the nature of your depression and the unique circumstances in your life.

How often do people go to therapy?

Some people begin by seeing a therapist quite frequently, perhaps every week. As improvement begins, they reduce the frequency to once every two to three weeks.

Do I have to understand the root cause of my depression before I can get better?

Understanding yourself is a lifelong process and you cannot gather all the insight you need in one course of psychotherapy. That doesn't mean you can't make progress and find ways to climb out of depression. In fact, it is sometimes only later, when you are stronger and on stable ground, that you can begin to fully understand the nature of your depression.

How do medications and psychotherapy fit together?

Antidepressant medications are intended to be used in conjunction with psychotherapy. Many people with depression are able to benefit from psychotherapy alone, without medication. But others need medication as well.

Often when people are using both kinds of treatments, therapy and medication, they see both a psychotherapist and a psychiatrist. They meet with a therapist relatively frequently, once every week or two, to gain a greater understanding of their depression and learn how to manage or improve their symptoms. They meet with a psychiatrist less frequently to have medication prescribed or adjusted. Ideally, all three people—the patient, the psychotherapist, and the psychiatrist—work together, exchanging information as treatment continues. Often people can stop taking the antidepressant as their depression lifts, but they continue seeing the therapist to deepen their understanding of themselves and their depression. Some psychiatrists play both roles—providing psychotherapy and prescribing medications—though this is becoming less common.

You may wish to discuss the question of medication with your psychotherapist. To learn more about antidepressant medication, see chapter 5.

WHAT CAN I DO TO HELP MYSELF?

1. Do you know anyone who is in psychotherapy? If you wanted to learn more about what psychotherapy is like, could you ask this

person some questions? Does this person find therapy helpful? In what ways? You do not need to tell this person that you are thinking of trying psychotherapy if it does not feel safe to do so.

2. What types of therapists are available in your community? Look in your phone book and start exploring. Is there a local mental health association or a chapter of the National Alliance of the Mentally Ill? Call your state psychological association or state psychiatric association to find out what kind of referral information they can give you.

3. Does your community have a local hotline for emotional problems? Sometimes talking to a stranger about your depression is good practice. You can begin to find words to describe what you are experiencing. And you can learn that people will accept you and listen to you.

CHAPTER 5

What Can I Do About My Depression?
Antidepressant Medication

Depression is not just an illness of the mind or the spirit. Depression is also an illness of the body. When people are depressed, the neuro-transmitters—the chemicals that carry messages between the nerve cells in the brain—may be affected. It isn't clear whether the chemical changes cause the depression or whether the depression causes the chemical changes; it may be different for different people. Regardless, medications that affect the neurotransmitters can be very important in bringing relief from depression.

People who are depressed may have many questions as they consider using antidepressants:

- What is antidepressant medication?
- How do I decide to use antidepressant medication?
- What is it like to be on antidepressant medication?
- What are the side effects of antidepressant medication?
- When and how do I stop taking antidepressant medication?

What Is Antidepressant Medication?

Antidepressants are medications that may help lift some of the darkness of depression. (Remember that depression includes a whole constellation of symptoms, not just feeling blue.) Antidepressants can take away some of the low mood and relieve the physical symptoms of depression such as sleep disruptions, appetite changes, and inability to concentrate. It's important to realize that antidepressants are not "uppers"; they don't make people happy or cheerful. And unlike uppers, antidepressants are not addictive. In the following pages, we will review the main types of antidepressants and explain how they work.

There are five main categories of antidepressants: monoamine oxidase inhibitors (MAO inhibitors or MAOIs), tricyclics, serotonin reuptake inhibitors (SSRIs), unique antidepressants, and mood stabilizers. We will begin with the older antidepressants.

Monoamine Oxidase Inhibitors

Monoamine oxidase inhibitors (MAOIs) include the drugs Parnate, Nardil, and Marplan. Originally developed to treat tuberculosis, MAOIs were found to also help alleviate depression among people who had both tuberculosis and depression. Since then, more effective drugs have been developed to treat tuberculosis. Drugs more effective in the treatment of most depressions have also been developed. However, since newer antidepressants aren't effective for every person, monoamine oxidase inhibitors are still used to treat depression that does not respond to other drugs.

How MAOIs Work

Monoamine oxidase inhibitors work by doing just what their name says they do: they stop the action of an enzyme called monoamine oxidase. Monoamine oxidase breaks down some important neurotransmitters in the brain, called amines. Amines include several neurotransmitters: serotonin, epinephrine, norepinephrine, and dopamine. Usually the monoamine oxidase enzyme is needed, because neurotransmitters need to be broken down in their own life cycle. However, according to the amine theory of depression, people who are depressed need all the amine neurotransmitters they can get. If oxidase is inhibited or stopped, more amines will be available in the brain.

Neurochemistry is difficult to follow, so here's an analogy that should make it a little easier to understand. Imagine you live in a house where you can toss your cardboard boxes down the stairs and someone magically flattens them and sends them out the back door for recycling. This system works so well, you never think twice about it. Then one day, you are packing for a big move and you need all the boxes you can get. As you toss them down the stairs, you say, "Save this box!" But the person at the bottom of the stairs knows how to do just one thing— flatten boxes. One solution is to send down a specialist, someone who can stop the box-flattener so the boxes can be saved for your use.

In this analogy, the boxes are the special neurotransmitters called amines. They start out whole, but are hurled across a space (in the brain, it's called a synapse) from one cell to another. Usually, the neurotransmitters need to be broken down. But in the case of depression, they're needed in their full form a while longer. To make sure this happens, an inhibitor is sent in to prevent them from being broken down.

Side Effects and Other Problems

MAOIs are not "first line" (the first recommended) antidepressants because of potential problems associated with their use. Physicians generally prescribe them only after other antidepressants have been tried. The main problem is that people taking MAOIs cannot eat or drink anything that contains the monoamine called *tyramine*. And tyramine is found in many common foods and beverages including aged cheeses, yogurt, canned food, alcohol, caffeine, and chocolate. Since the medication MAOI doesn't differentiate between what kinds of amines it allows to build up, tyramine builds up in the body if a person consumes these foods or beverages. Tyramine affects blood pressure. If a person's tyramine levels increase too much, blood pressure can suddenly increase, which in its most extreme state can cause death.

Despite their risks, MAOIs are effective antidepressants for many people. If other antidepressants have not worked, MAOIs may be prescribed, and people taking them must simply limit their diet. Their doctor can provide them with a comprehensive list of foods to avoid.

Note that because of the relatively low margin of safety with these drugs, they are generally not prescribed for addicts, who may be at risk for relapse to alcohol or other drug use.

Tricyclics

Tricyclics were first developed in the late 1950s and early 1960s. Common names of the different types of tricyclics include Tofranil, Elavil, Asendin, Aventyl, and Sinequan. Norpramine (desipramine) is a later version. Tricyclics produce many therapeutic effects, including improved appetite, sleep, and mood. It generally takes two to four weeks before these medications begin to take effect. People may feel sedated and sleepy before they begin to experience the benefits of the drug. Research generally shows high success rates with tricyclics; 60 to 70 percent of people who are depressed improve with tricyclics.

How Tricyclics Work

Tricyclic antidepressants work by blocking the re-uptake of various neurotransmitters in the brain, especially serotonin and norepinephrine. Theorists believe that a certain amount of these neurotransmitters is needed in the synapses between the cells. If the amount becomes too low, the theory goes, depression occurs. Blocking their re-uptake ensures that more of the neurotransmitter will be available between the cells.

As an analogy, imagine a game in which the object is to keep at least forty basketballs in motion. A thrower tosses basketballs into the middle of a gym. Some of the balls are red, some blue, some green, and some yellow. A catcher grabs the balls and puts them in baskets. There are extra points for keeping the blue and red balls in motion. But pretty soon, hardly any balls are left in the open area of the gym! No matter how hard the thrower works, the ball catcher is never far behind.

In this analogy, the thrower and catcher are special cells in the brain, neurons, that are responsible for transporting the neurotransmitters. The basketballs are the different kinds of neurotransmitters, and the red and blue balls are norepinephrine and serotonin. One solution is for the thrower to hire someone else to come into the gym and stop the ball catcher from picking up so many balls, especially the red and blue balls. This will keep more of them in motion. Theorists believe that tricyclics serve this function. They block the re-uptake of neurotransmitters, especially norepinephirine and serotonin.

Side Effects and Other Problems

Tricyclics have one major downfall—their side effects. These include dry mouth, urinary retention, constipation, drowsiness, fast heart rate, and dizziness when standing up quickly (which happens because blood pressure drops too quickly). In addition, sexual desire and performance may be diminished. Many people are able to live with the side effects; for other people, the side effects are extreme or intolerable. These people may not be able to experience the benefits of tricyclics because they stop taking the drug or they take it in lower doses than are recommended.

The negative side effects of antidepressants have been a significant problem for a long time. The search is on for an antidepressant without such side effects. The first drug of that kind is Prozac, one of a new family of antidepressants called selective serotonin re-uptake inhibitors.

Selective Serotonin Re-Uptake Inhibitors

The public's thinking about depression and antidepressants has been revolutionized by the selective serotonin re-uptake inhibitors (SSRIs) including Prozac, Zoloft, and Paxil. In 1987, Prozac became the first in this family to be approved by the Food and Drug Administration. Prozac must generally be taken for about two to six weeks before it reaches peak effectiveness. However, some people notice benefits within the first week. The first changes are often subtle decreases in anxiety and sadness; often friends of the person who is depressed notice the changes even before the person taking the medication does.

Prozac has claimed an enormous amount of public attention. Over eleven thousand patients around the world have been involved in studies of Prozac, and over three thousand articles about the drug have been published in medical and scientific journals.[1] Several popular books have been written about it, including the national best-seller *Listening to Prozac*. Prozac has also been the cover story for *Time* and *Newsweek*.

With all the media attention—and personal testimonials at dinner parties—people often assume that Prozac's success rates must far surpass earlier antidepressants. Surprisingly, recent comparison studies have shown that Prozac is no more effective than the older antidepressants in the tricyclic family, such as Elavil and Tofranil. Researchers at the State University of New York reviewed thirteen published studies of Prozac.[2] They compared the results of these studies with studies of other types of antidepressants and found that the results of Prozac were roughly comparable to those of other antidepressants.[3] The researchers found that about two-thirds of the people experienced a significant reduction in their depression with Prozac. Unfortunately, another 20 percent of the patients in the study dropped out because they did not like the side effects they felt with Prozac. These figures are similar to what researchers report about tricyclics.

What does this mean? First, it means that Prozac is not a wonder drug; it does not help everyone. Second, some people experience side effects that dissuade them from continuing to use Prozac. However, negative side effects are not as big a problem with Prozac as with the older antidepressants. Only about half as many people have to stop taking Prozac because of negative side effects as do people who have to stop taking tricyclic medications.[4] Third—and this is what has made Prozac so popular—a large number of people are able to take Prozac, experience a decrease in depression, and have only mild or no side effects. Because of this, far more people are willing to try Prozac or one of the other newer antidepressants.

How SSRIs work

One characteristic of serotonin re-uptake inhibitors sets them apart from all other antidepressants. SSRIs block the re-uptake of only *one* of the brain's neurotransmitters, serotonin. SSRIs work by maintaining the natural level of serotonin between cells of the brain. In this way they are very "clean"; they affect only serotonin. The other antidepressants, tricyclics and MAOIs, affect other brain chemicals in addition to serotonin. Why does this matter? It seems that the more specific the action on the neurotransmitters, the fewer the side effects. The fewer the side effects, the easier antidepressants are for people to take. Antidepressants can only work if people are able to take them regularly for a certain period of time, usually at least a few months.

Because SSRIs tend to have fewer side effects, they are used by many psychiatrists as "first line" antidepressants. This means that an SSRI is the first drug psychiatrists generally recommend when they diagnose a person as depressed. Prozac and other SSRIs are also recommended often for people who have tried other antidepressants without success. Doctors find that more than half of these people are helped with the newer medications.[5]

Side Effects and Other Problems

People tend to have less trouble with SSRIs than with other antidepressants. Still, some people do experience side effects. These can include nausea or diarrhea, abdominal distress, headaches, nervousness, and sleep problems.

The media has also called attention to another concern: does Prozac transform personalities? The verdict is generally no. People with dysthymia who have been depressed for much of their lives may seem to be transformed when depression has lifted. Depression causes a person to be withdrawn, irritable, and unhappy. When treated, the same person will be more gregarious and easygoing. This is less a transformation of personality than a decrease in depression.

Using SSRIs for Other Disorders

The balance of serotonin in the brain may be important for disorders besides depression—including alcoholism, obsessive compulsive disorder, panic disorder, and eating disorders. Because people who have these problems also often experience depression, physicians may prescribe Prozac, Paxil, or Zoloft (or other types of SSRIs, as they become available) for these patients. These medications are apt to help the depression and may also help the other problem.

Unique Antidepressants

There are three newer antidepressants that don't fit in the categories discussed above: Effexor, Desyrel, and Serzone.

Effexor affects both serotonin and norepinephrine, as the tricyclics do, but in a way that does not cause as many side effects. Overall,

Effexor appears to have fewer side effects than Prozac and the other SSRIs. Even so, about 19 percent of all people taking Effexor stop because of side effects, usually because of problems like nausea, insomnia, drowsiness, or increased blood pressure at high doses.

Desyrel and Serzone are in the same family of antidepressants. Unlike Effexor, they affect only serotonin. Like Effexor, their side effects are more tolerable for most people than the tricyclics.

Mood Stabilizers

Special medications are used for treating bipolar disorders. These include lithium and Tegretol. Both are quite effective but very different from each other. Lithium is used solely in the treatment of manic episodes and depression. Tegretol was initially designed to reduce or prevent convulsions; it also works against certain kinds of nerve pain. More recently Tegretol has been found to be a good alternative medication for some people with bipolar disorder.

Mood stabilizers are typically started when people have their first manic episode, or when they are experiencing a depressive episode and have a history of manic episodes. These medications help level a person's mood to a more steady state, which can help prevent future episodes.

How Do I Decide Whether to Use
Antidepressant Medication?

If you've read this chapter so far, you know something about antidepressants and how they work. But this doesn't answer the question, *Are they for me?* Imagine going to a therapist for an evaluation of your depression and the therapist says, "I'd like you to consider taking an antidepressant medication." How do you decide what to do? How do people make this kind of decision?

Many people have fears about taking medication. For instance, people think taking medication is a sign of weakness. Erica worried that if she took antidepressants it would mean she wasn't strong enough. She had always thought of herself as a happy person leading a stable, secure life. But her world came crashing down after a divorce. She attempted suicide. After this, she joined a women's support group and went back to work. Erica struggled for four years before she decided to see a therapist. At this point she had many issues she wanted to work on. But Erica was surprised when her therapist talked to her about depression and suggested she might want to consider using antidepressants.

> *I hated the idea of medication. I really felt that taking meds meant that I had failed somehow, that if I were just strong enough, or just good enough, or just whatever enough, I wouldn't need drugs. It was certainly okay that other people needed meds; it didn't mean there was anything wrong with them, but it was not okay for me. To me, it meant that I was weak and disgusting. Even though I knew that thinking was flawed, I couldn't stop feeling that way. But I decided to go ahead and try the meds anyway.*

Erica was relieved when the medication she took helped her get better. But the decision to take antidepressants wasn't easy for her. She didn't know many people who were taking antidepressants—except her mother, which did not make her decision easier. She had seen her mother's depression as a sign of weakness and didn't want to see the same thing in herself.

All people have a time when they look in the mirror and see one of their parents. For most people this can be disconcerting, no matter what characteristic is reflected back. But when people see a characteristic they don't like, it can be especially hard. If there has been something about their parents that troubles them, they may have sworn they'd never be like that. For instance, a person might have sworn *I'll never yell at my kids like my dad yelled at me* or *I'm not going to worry constantly like my mom did.* The same phenomenon can happen with depression. If a person's parents were depressed, that person may have promised to be more positive, more active, more appreciative, and less dour and unhappy. This was similar to how Erica felt. Her mother had been depressed for many years, and Erica thought she lacked willpower and initiative—mentally weak. Erica promised herself she would never be weak like her mother. Now her mother was finally taking antidepressants, and Erica herself was being confronted with a diagnosis of depression and a recommendation to take antidepressants!

Erica had to make a decision about her life. If she continued to see her mother as weak, she would probably reject the idea that she, herself, was depressed and needed medications. It would be too deflating to be in the same category. On the other hand, a diagnosis of depression might help Erica see her mother—and herself—with new eyes. Maybe her mother was doing the best she could with her depression. Perhaps it wasn't her mother's fault she was depressed. In turn, Erica might be able to see herself with some compassion.

Erica was able to choose to see both herself and her mother with new eyes. Over time, Erica was able to use this experience as another way to find her own identity. Yes, she realized, she had depression too; but this did not mean that she "was" her mother.

Brent also had trouble with the idea of taking medications. He had been in therapy for two years, and while his recovery from an eating disorder was going well, his depression wasn't improving.

> My therapist recommended I try antidepressants. He could see that no matter how hard I was working, I wasn't getting over my depression. I didn't really like the idea, but I went to the psychiatrist he recommended. The psychiatrist did a twenty-minute interview and suggested imipramine. At first I did not get the prescription filled, thinking it was given too easily. How did the psychiatrist really know I needed medications? I carried the slip of paper with the prescription around with me and felt like I had a snake in my pocket. Weeks went by. But my depression got worse and my therapist encouraged me to try the antidepressant. Finally I got the prescription filled, and it did help, though I had a lot of side effects . . . my mouth was dry, and I felt really sedated. The worst thing was decreased sexual ability. I went back to the psychiatrist, and he gave me a prescription for Prozac.

> When the psychiatrist gave me the prescription, I agonized over the idea of taking medications. Taking them just confirmed my diagnosis of depression, and I felt weak and ashamed about that. I knew that if the antidepressants did work, I'd feel guilty about needing them. But I did take them, because I was even more afraid of the depression.

Brent's experience raises an important point: there is generally no rush to take antidepressants. This can be a good route to follow if the depression is not life-threatening or severe. You can take some time to learn some things about yourself and establish a trusting relationship with a therapist. Then if you do decide with your therapist that medication might be helpful, you have already established good groundwork. And if the antidepressants help with the depression, you've got someone to help you celebrate the changes and build on the successes. Medication does not take the place of seeing a therapist, but it may be another useful way to treat your depression.

How long you wait before taking antidepressants is something that you and your therapist can discuss. It depends on the severity of depression and the progress made without them. If the depression is not interfering greatly with everyday life, and you are making improvements, you may not need medications. If, on the other hand, depression is threatening your will to live, you may want to consider antidepressants right away.

Brent had tried for two years to overcome his depression without medication. Some might say he didn't need to wait this long. But there were two factors in operation here:

- He was working with a therapist and seeing some progress. He maintained hope that he could rise out of the depression fully. He needed the time to see that therapy alone was not going to alleviate his depression. But that does not mean at all that his two years in therapy were wasted. He had learned a lot in therapy that helped him in his struggle with depression. The medications were just another part of his treatment. And Brent took antidepressants for a relatively short period of time (about a year). They gave him the boost he needed, and he's been well for many years since without them.
- Brent was quite determined to overcome depression without medications. For many people, having control and a sense of mastery is important. There's nothing that says you "should" take medications. When the time came for Brent to consider medications, he had learned what he could and could not do on his own to reduce his depression.

Brent's story raises another important point. He was very thoughtful about his decision to take medications. He legitimately asked whether a psychiatrist who didn't know him well could determine his need for medications. Because there is no exact way to diagnose and treat depression—it doesn't show up on an x ray—people may find it especially difficult and especially important to trust the psychiatrist who prescribes their medication. Although this was difficult for Brent, he did have some reasons to trust that taking antidepressants was the right decision. He trusted the therapist who referred him to the psychiatrist for antidepressants. After two years of working with him, Brent felt confident his therapist knew him well. He could also trust his own knowledge. He knew he was depressed and stuck. Even though he wasn't sure about the physician from just one meeting, he was able to accept the medication because he could trust his own knowledge and his relationship with his therapist.

What if you are in a situation where you do not have a therapist or anyone else to help you make this decision? Or, what if you are just beginning to recognize your depression?

Here are some guidelines to use in making the decision about whether to try antidepressants as part of your treatment for depression.

1. Remember that taking medications is just one part of the work you'll need to do to overcome or live with depression. Some people get so focused on the medication question that it gets "bigger than life."

2. You need to have confidence in the physician you see. Feel free to ask as many questions as needed to gain that confidence.

3. Usually, there should be no rush to take antidepressants. If you don't believe that medication is the path for you, don't feel pressured into it—unless, of course, you realize that you're at a point in your depression where you need to let others make some decisions. Even if antidepressants are suggested and you choose not to take them, keep working with a therapist on your depression. Together, you can decide at a later date if you need to revisit the question of medications.

4. Remember that many medications have side effects and risks (pages 93–95 and the appendix describes these). Some medications may have side effects that are intolerable to you. Some medications for depression or anxiety should not be used by recovering people. If you are recovering from addiction, take the physical consequences of your disease into consideration. Also, if you have a history of liver damage or seizures, be sure to tell your physician. Some medications will not be appropriate or you will need a smaller dose.

WHAT IS IT LIKE TO TAKE ANTIDEPRESSANT MEDICATION?

You may wonder, *Will I still be "me" if I take an antidepressant? Will it give me some sort of high? Will it just make me oblivious to my problems?*

The answer to all of these questions is no. Antidepressants do not change people or make them high or oblivious to their problems. In fact, many people who have taken antidepressants describe it as something that doesn't change their life directly. Rather, they say antidepressants provide a stable foundation so that they can make changes. Melvin Konner wrote an article for *The New York Times Magazine* about depression and antidepressants, using his own experience as a point of reference. He said, "For me the medicine became a platform on which I could function in a very different way."[6]

Tanya did not become a different person when she took antidepressants, but she was able to cope with her problems easier. Like Brent, Tanya had been depressed for a long time and had been working with a therapist. When her therapist suggested taking medications, she thought a long time before deciding to try them. At the same time, she continued attending a support group and seeing her therapist. When asked if the medications made any difference, she said:

> Yes. I saw things were a little better. I seemed to be more tolerant of others and less judgmental of myself, and I felt like I was making pretty good decisions. I could think so much better. I immediately started doing better in the college classes I was taking. But the most astounding thing was how the people in my life saw the improvement. Comments came from

people who didn't even know I was on meds—my boss, for instance, although he still pushed my buttons and I still dreaded going to work every day. But there was a difference—sometimes I was actually able to let things roll off my back for real, not just pretend to. I don't mean to say that it was a huge difference, that everything was just rosy, but it was different. I could handle things better.

Tanya seemed to become more resilient. As she admits herself, the problems didn't go away. She still had a job she didn't like; her boss was still insensitive; college was still demanding. But with the changes occurring within her, the problems affected her less. She could use her energy to continue her personal growth, rather than battle the world.

After a while, Tanya quit her job and started her own business. She said with justifiable pride, "My ex-boss is currently my biggest client!" When people are depressed, they often stay in intolerable situations, mostly because they don't have the energy to make changes. Obtaining some relief from depression often creates a window of opportunity for people to let go of old ways of living and begin new healthier ways. Tanya is able to look back now and say:

Through my passage of recovery from depression, I experience life on life's terms. I go through my ups and downs, but they are normal, everyday ups and downs; not exaggerated ups and downs. After being diagnosed with depression, getting therapy, and taking medication, I have an emotionally stable life that I never dreamed possible.

The path ahead of Tanya may not be easy. Managing her own business requires a great deal of self-discipline, which has been a problem for her in the past. She also misses the stimulation of taking college classes. Plus, she sometimes wonders if some of the symptoms of depression may be recurring. But Tanya is staying on the path. She's facing everyday problems of living and resolving them. She's also learning to recognize and deal with depression. She continues to see her therapist and go to her support group. Tanya has a good foundation for continuing her climb out of depression.

Taking antidepressants also gave Paul the stability he needed to deal with his problems. Paul had been depressed for so long that he thought his days free of depression were brief manic episodes. Life without depression was a new experience for him.

> *I experienced relief from the depression within four days of taking Prozac. I began experiencing what I had formerly labeled mania on a daily basis and now realize that it is life without depression. I found everyday tasks, such as cleaning my house and getting myself ready for work, easier. I started exercising, taking a good long walk almost every day. I haven't yet experienced the depression I had before. I occasionally experience some symptoms if I get overly tired or have a stretch of stressful days. Even when life gets hard, the Prozac helps keep me steady enough to deal with the problems. The problems in my life got a lot worse for a couple of years—but I didn't consider suicide. I went through some disastrous relationships with women; my daughter went through a difficult adolescence; I failed some important exams for work, lost my job, and incurred huge financial problems from being unemployed. But with Prozac, I didn't die.*

Being on medications did not transport Paul to a fairyland. Paul had a lot of problems to face—he had to learn how to develop healthy relationships with women, how to deal with his teenage daughter as she raged through adolescence, and how to go on when doors closed on his chosen career path. But the key fact was that he was able to walk through the depression and stay alive. He could do what he needed to do to stay on the path.

Now Paul has made some satisfying changes in his life. "A year ago I remarried and opened a business. I am happier now than I have ever been in my life." Paul saw his career problems as an opportunity and found new ways to use his talents. No doubt he will still bring some of his old issues to his new relationship, but he's learned what they are and can talk about them openly. He's not ashamed of who he is; instead, he's grateful for the support he's had and the wisdom he's gained.

Anthea found that taking antidepressants reduced the symptoms of her depression enough that she could take a fresh look at her problems. She had struggled with dysthymia and episodes of depression for years, and was reluctant to take any kind of medication. She was self-reliant and thought if she just worked hard enough at her depression, she could get through it. She first took Tofranil, one of the earlier tricyclics, and was somewhat disappointed with the results. It diminished her depression, but the side effects were so aggravating she couldn't enjoy the result. She went back to her doctor and was given a prescription for one of the newer antidepressants, Prozac.

> *Prozac did just what the other antidepressant did, but without the side effects. In fact, I didn't feel anything when I took Prozac. For me, it was just like taking aspirin. No side effects—and no jolt of good feelings. But something happened. Somehow, it lifted me over the void. The void, the abyss, was still there. But I didn't get sucked into it anymore. I could somehow—just somehow—let myself be carried over it. I had a feeling I needed to come back to the abyss someday, but it could wait until I was stronger. For now, what I needed was just to get to the other side of it. All my negative thoughts just weren't there. Bad things, hard things, still happened, but I could deal with them without tumbling into that black hole.*

Anthea still had plenty of things to work on. Prozac didn't take that away. And it didn't take away her conviction that there were deep places within herself that she needed to explore. But during depression, the most important task is to stay alive and get through life's everyday dilemmas.

Raul battled dysthymia with occasional periods of full-blown depression. He was well educated, and because of his intelligence and likability, Raul often landed high-level, responsible positions. But every time he was able to put together a period of stability, it seemed to fall apart. His self-esteem was plummeting, and he began to seriously consider suicide. After realizing that he couldn't stop the slide by himself, he began seeing a therapist and started medications.

> *My personal opinion is that the medication saved my life. I do not take it to get happy, but to get out of bed. It does not solve my problems, but gives me the strength to tackle the problems. It puts a floor under me below which I cannot sink. The floor, for the first time in my life, is the same as everybody else's floor.*

With all of these success stories, a person could get the idea that taking antidepressants works for everyone. Unfortunately, this isn't true. For many, success takes more than medication; it also takes months, or even years, of hard work in therapy and self-help groups. At one point, Taylor hit a rough spot in her recovery. Reflecting on the role of medication in resolving her depression, she said:

> *Meds won't cure you by themselves. You are still responsible for your actions or lack of actions. And it's still difficult to do the things you need to do for yourself. I still need to go to meetings; I still need to work the Steps; I still need to call my friends and my sponsor. I know I haven't been doing those things and I'm not doing too well as a result. Maybe meds can help, but just like anything else, it only works when you work it. (I hate it when God talks to me through my own mouth!)*

Taylor could reflect on her situation with some humor. She took the medications, started to climb out of the hole of depression, and could see that there was hope for her life. But, as pointed out in so many of the stories, she still had hard work ahead.

Some people get little or no relief from one antidepressant and may need to work with their physician over a period of time to find a different antidepressant, or combination of medications, that helps. For others, the side effects don't outweigh the benefits. Still others simply feel no different on medications and decide that this route is not for them. Antidepressants are not magic pills. But as shown by the stories in this chapter, they give many people the foundation they need to cope with life's difficulties.

What Are the Side Effects of Antidepressant Medication?

Antidepressants, just like any other medication, have their down sides. Depending on the type of medication, side effects can range from inconvenient to life-threatening. Most of the time, and for most people, the side effects are minor compared to living with the depression. But it's important to know what the expected side effects are for any medication prescribed.

There are common, or expected, side effects with each of the different medications. Whether the side effect appears, and how prominent it is, depends on the medication and the person taking it.

Tricyclics often have some of the following side effects.[7]

Side Effects	*What to Do*
Dry mouth	Drink lots of water, chew gum, suck on hard candy.
Constipation	Eat bran cereals, prunes, and other fruits and vegetables. Exercise.
Bladder problems (difficulty emptying bladder)	Call your physician if you experience pain or if this side effect is interfering with your daily life.
Sexual problems (increased or decreased interest in sex, or increase in time required to experience an orgasm. Men may not be able to maintain erections.)	See a physician if these problems interfere with daily life.
Blurred vision	See a physician if this does not pass soon. It can occur when you first begin antidepressants.
Dizziness when rising from a sitting or lying position	Rise more slowly when getting up from a chair or bed. Sit on the edge of a chair or bed for a moment before standing up. The dizziness, which is due to a quick drop in blood pressure when getting up from a chair or bed, is called *orthostatic hypotension*. If it continues and interferes with daily life, talk to a physician.
Drowsiness	Do not drive or operate heavy equipment if you feel groggy or sedated. This usually passes within two weeks.
Weight gain	Ask your doctor if you can switch to a different medication.

Most of the newer antidepressants in the category of SSRIs do not produce the side effects listed on page 94. However, they have side effects of their own.[8]

Side Effects	What to Do
Nausea/diarrhea	See a physician if this does not pass within two to three weeks.
Abdominal distress	Try taking antacids and antiflatullents. These can be bought without prescriptions.
Headaches	See a physician if this problem does not go away soon.
Nervousness/agitation	See a physician if this does not stop during the first few weeks.
Sleep problems (insomnia or drowsiness)	See a physician if sleep patterns do not improve within a few weeks. Sleep is also affected by depression, so it's best to wait a few weeks on medication to see if sleep patterns improve.

Differing Responses to Side Effects

Everyone responds to antidepressants a little differently. Anthea's experience, mentioned earlier in this chapter, illustrates two extremes. She could not tolerate the side effects she had on Tofranil. Her depression was lifting, but the medication decreased her ability to be sexual. When her doctor switched her medication to Prozac, she experienced no side effects. On one medication, Anthea's side effects were significant; on another medication, they were absent. Some people are afraid to talk to their doctor about side effects, thinking they should be able to tolerate them. Anthea's story illustrates the importance of asking questions and speaking up when things don't seem right.

Other people have different experiences. Although antidepressants helped Bonnie, she wasn't sure in the beginning if the side effects were tolerable.

The side effects were mostly diarrhea—the first day was hell. But after about three days, everything went pretty much back to normal. My sex drive decreased at first. But after about four or five months it seemed to come back, maybe not completely, but I'm thirty-eight years old, so I'm sliding down the wrong side of that "sexual peak" thing anyway.

Bonnie's libido, or sexual interest, may have started to return after four or five months because her depression was clearing. Her body may have also been adjusting to the medication. Over time, she may want to review how the medication may be affecting her sex drive. Age does not necessarily mean a person experiences diminished interest in sexual activity. It's possible that a lower dose or a different medication may help Bonnie regain her full libido. She will decide if and when this is an important consideration for her.

It took some time for Arnette to find a combination of medications that worked for her. And in the process, she gained weight. The more typical side effect of the newer antidepressants is weight loss. But as Arnette's story points out, different people have different side effects. It's best to talk openly about them and come to terms with them.

> *I gained ten pounds a year for two years during the course of taking Tegretol, Pamelor, Depakote, and Zoloft. I complained about it to my doctor, explaining that taking medication for depression and gaining weight from it can make a depressed person depressed! He did say that taking the medication was a double-edged sword. So what is one to do? Be happy and fat . . . or depressed and skinny? Not much choice. The medicine makes me crave sweets, which is unusual for me. I don't usually like sugar.*

Arnette decided to quit the medications altogether and she lost weight. After two months, she was happy about her slim figure, but symptoms of severe depression started to return. Arnette recognized that the benefits of managing her depression far exceeded the disappointment of weight gain. She went back to her doctor and started a different combination of medications. She made sure she exercised, tried to eat healthy foods, and decided to live with any weight gain she might have. For most people, five pounds a year are not life threatening.

A person with an eating disorder may not be able to stay on track with weight changes so easily. In that case, a different medication, redoubled commitment to Overeaters Anonymous or another self-help group, and therapy for symptoms of bulimia, anorexia, or compulsive overeating may be needed.

Some people sleep more when they begin taking antidepressants, and some find their sleep disrupted. Jennifer found she had sleep problems when she first started taking Prozac: "I initially experienced some sleep interruption, but that passed within a few weeks. That was the only side effect I noticed." Others notice that they dream more or have more vivid dreams. Increased dreaming may be due in part to the depression lifting and in part to the medication. But sleep problems, especially during the first few weeks of taking antidepressants, are not unusual. This seems to be more true for the SSRIs and the other newer antidepressants. The important fact to remember is that this side effect typically subsides.

Sometimes, though very infrequently, people taking antidepressants will find that their brain chemistry has been adjusted too far in the opposite direction, triggering a manic episode. When this happens, they become agitated, can't sleep, have a tremendous amount of energy, and feel euphoric. Some people have trouble discerning the difference between feeling normal and moving into a manic episode. If you experience any of these symptoms, it is important to contact your physician.

The side effects we have been discussing so far are relatively mild. Although quite rare, some severe reactions can also occur. Here is a list of considerations that anyone taking antidepressants should be aware of:

- The older types of medications, tricyclics and MAO inhibitors, can cause changes in blood pressure and heart rhythms.
- A few of the antidepressants lower the seizure threshold. This means that someone prone to seizures, or with a history of them, may start to have seizures when antidepressant medication is taken.
- With all antidepressants, it is important that the liver and kidneys are functioning reasonably well in order to metabolize the medications.

- No long-term studies have been done to determine the overall effect of antidepressants on the body. People have stayed on antidepressants for years, and to date, no obvious problems have been seen. Still, no one knows for sure that long-term use will not have negative effects on the body.

Potential serious problems, along with the fact that the effects of long-term use are unknown, make it important to work closely with, and ask questions of, your doctor.

Combining alcohol and other drugs with antidepressant medication can produce severe problems. With most antidepressants, use of alcohol and other drugs is strongly discouraged. In itself, alcohol is a depressant and not a logical beverage for someone who is struggling to overcome depression. Beyond that, the combination of alcohol and other drugs with antidepressants can be dangerous.

- When a person is on MAO inhibitors, wine and beer can cause a dramatic increase in blood pressure and, potentially, death.
- Tricyclics and MAO inhibitors enhance the effect of alcohol and other drugs. This means that they interact with alcohol and drugs and magnify their effect in unpredictable ways.
- The newer antidepressants such as Prozac do not seem to interact with alcohol and other drugs in the same way that other antidepressants do. However, caution is still advised.

WHEN AND HOW DO I STOP TAKING ANTIDEPRESSANT MEDICATION?

After taking antidepressants for a while, a person will want to know, *When should I stop taking them?* There seem to be two main paths that people follow with antidepressants. Some people need them for a relatively short period of time, a year or less; others find they need to remain on them indefinitely. And some people who take antidepressants for a short time return to them later in life if depression recurs. Let's take a look at short-term and long-term use.

Short-Term Use of Antidepressants

Some people take antidepressants for a short time, six to twelve months, and are able to get back on track. It takes about two months for most antidepressants to fully take effect and stabilize in a person's body. Then it can take another period of time, at least four more months, for the person to incorporate all the changes that come with being less depressed. A person needs time to learn to live *without* depression and to be able to sustain that state confidently before discontinuing medication.

People who can benefit from short-term antidepressant therapy are often those who are experiencing a major depression for the first time or have most of the symptoms of a major depression—difficulties with sleeping, eating, anxiety, concentration, and low mood. The trigger is most likely to be external or social—job loss or break up of a relationship. Depression is quite alien for these people. They are not used to being depressed; it is not their usual state of mind.

Bert Pepper, M.D., noted anecdotally in a conversation with the author in December 1994, that half of the patients that he saw strictly for medication monitoring (in contrast to psychotherapy) needed medication for less than six months. These patients continued on with their psychotherapy, but a relatively brief course of medications got them through a period when they were stuck in depression. Dr. Pepper sees the six-month medication period broken down into two months to get stable and an additional four months to incorporate behavioral changes and make adjustments.

Beth's depression came suddenly after a series of setbacks in her career. Once a vibrant, active, outgoing woman, she lost all confidence and self-esteem, became withdrawn, barely ate, and was having difficulty sleeping. When she was near suicide, she went to a psychiatrist, certain that she was in a hole so deep she'd never get out.

> *I took Paxil for about eight months. My psychiatrist assured me that my depression could be turned around and that I could be "jump started" within a few months on the medication. I was very skeptical. Now, four months without Paxil, I feel as fine and stable and serene as I did while on*

it. I have read a great deal about that family of drugs [SSRIs], and I am convinced that taking it was the correct thing to do.

After she was stabilized on antidepressants, Beth got back on a regular program of exercise, her relationship with her partner improved, and she regained her confidence. Beth needed antidepressants for only a short time.

Mike looked back and realized that he'd experienced depression pretty regularly during the winter. (This type of depression is known as *seasonal affective disorder.*) He had learned to live with this, almost to expect it. But he wasn't prepared for what happened to him when his marriage broke down. His self-esteem crashed and he couldn't think well or make decisions. He wasn't sleeping or eating, and he seriously considered suicide. This depression went on for months, longer and more severe than any he had experienced before. Finally, he saw a psychologist and started individual therapy to work on some important issues surrounding his divorce, and he was referred to a psychiatrist for medications. The physician recommended Zoloft, which he took for about nine months.

The first thing I noticed was that I was able to concentrate. This started within the first week of taking medication. As the weeks went on, I felt my self-esteem improving. Now I'm much more optimistic about life—about my life. I still get the seasonal blues, but even that isn't as bad and I recognize it for what it is. (I mostly get slowed down and sleep a lot.) But the sense of worthlessness and hopelessness is gone. And I don't think about suicide. I'm not sure how it happened, but Zoloft almost seems to have triggered a permanent change in my brain chemistry. Or maybe it just gave me my first glimpse of a normal, healthy, positive outlook on life and its possibilities.

Mike, too, got a "jump start" out of his depression. He still had things to work on—for example, he knew he was still feeling grief about his divorce and needed to look at what part he might have played in it—but now he could do that with clear eyes.

While many people only need to take antidepressants for a few months, it's important not to quit prematurely. Some people quit taking their medications just when they begin to feel better, thinking they don't need them anymore. But if they quit before they have really made the needed adjustments, they may sink back into depression.

Barry had been depressed off and on for years, and was in the midst of a custody battle for his three children. He had also lost his job. He wasn't sleeping or eating well, and his fatigue and inability to concentrate only added to his feelings of worthlessness. He did start to see a social worker for therapy and then a psychiatrist for medications, but he stopped both when his depression started to lift. The depression got unbearable again, and he went back to therapy and medication. Soon, this became a pattern. He said tearfully:

> I don't really like to continue taking medication and seeing a therapist because I want to get on with my life. I don't really believe in all this stuff anyway. I'm the type that always thought people who said they were depressed were just copping out. Besides, I'm afraid the judge will hold it against me if he sees I'm in therapy and on medication. I might not get custody of my kids.

Barry has some difficult choices to make. Clearly, he feels so much shame about his depression that it is difficult for him to accept help. He may also have reasonable fears about how decisions are sometimes made about child custody. But without treatment for depression, Barry was going to stay stuck in a very bleak place. He knew that if he stayed depressed, he wasn't going to be able to take care of his kids even if he did obtain custody of them. And without being able to work, he couldn't support them. Neither option was good. Ultimately, Barry decided to renew his efforts with therapy and medication, and to stay committed to that path. It's difficult to know how long Barry will need to stay on medication, but if he can put together four to twelve months of solid time on them, he may then be able to try tapering off. With the help of his doctor, he can monitor his depression and decide when to stop taking medication.

Jack also had second thoughts about continuing his medication. He didn't want to take them in the first place, and after about nine months, he decided he was better and didn't refill his prescription.

> *I didn't give it much thought. I just knew that they cost a lot and that I didn't like taking them. It wasn't that I had any side effects—I didn't. It was because taking them kept reminding me that I had a psychiatric illness.*

After about two months of being off medications, Jack could feel himself slipping into depression again. He talked to his therapist, and they both agreed it would be better if he got back on the antidepressants. He also continued his self-help program and therapy sessions, and was able to discontinue his medications with the support of his therapist in just six more months. Several years have passed, and though life has thrown him many challenges, Jack has not needed medications again.

Long-Term Use of Antidepressants

Because few long-term research studies have been done with antidepressants, not much is known about the way long-term use affects the body. It's possible that negative side effects will show up. Therefore, most physicians plan for their patients to stop using antidepressants at some point. However, some people find that they are at such high risk for recurring depression that going off medications is intolerable. For many of these people, it is not just a matter of having a better life; it is a matter of having a life worth living. This was Virginia's experience.

Virginia had been depressed for most of her life when she sought help for her severe depression. After three years and after remarkable progress through the depths of depression, she moved to a new city and started working with a new physician. Reasonably, the physician suggested a trial of time off medications.

> *He suggested that I begin decreasing my dosage from one capsule a day to three per week and ultimately cease taking Prozac. I attempted to follow his advice, but within six weeks I was experiencing some vague depression. I also had trouble concentrating and couldn't seem to stop myself from overeating. I talked to my doctor about these symptoms, and we agreed that I'd start taking the Prozac every day again. Within a few days, the symptoms disappeared. I don't plan to stop taking Prozac.*

Because the effects of taking antidepressants long term are not known, Virginia's wish to continue taking Prozac is understandable. She and her physician may want to review the need for medication at a later date. The key issue is that Virginia is working closely with her physician and understands herself well enough to know what is working for her.

People with long histories of depression, with recurrent depression, or who are older when they have their first episode may be at greater risk for another depressive episode. John Greden, a psychiatrist, uses the following rule of thumb when trying to determine whether a person is likely to have another onset of depression. He says that (a) if people experience depression for the first time at age fifty or older; (b) if they have had at least two episodes after the age of forty; or (c) if they have had at least three episodes at any time in their lives, they are likely to experience depression again.[9] Still, this isn't true for everyone. Some people fit in one of these categories but will never experience another bout of depression.

People who have a high risk for recurrent depression may need to stay on antidepressant medication indefinitely. A group of researchers at the University of Pittsburgh School of Medicine studied twenty patients who had a history of recurrent depression. All had been taking Tofranil for at least three years and were free from major depressive symptoms. With the patients' permission, half of them continued on Tofranil and half were given placebos. The patients did not know which they were receiving; both pills looked alike. Of those who were on Tofranil, only one experienced an episode of depression. But two-thirds of those on placebos had a depressive episode. In reviewing the results, the researchers concluded that people with a history of repeated episodes of depression less than two and one-half years apart should stay on a maintenance dose of antidepressants for at least five years.

Remember that these findings about who is at high risk for relapse to depression are generalizations: they may or may not apply to you. If you fit the criteria, you won't necessarily experience depression again, but it is something to consider. If you are at high risk, you may want to continue with antidepressants and make sure you are taking other action to help stave off depression. The good news is that even if you are at high risk for repeated depression, effective treatment is available.

Long-term use of medication is also necessary for people with bipolar disorder. They generally need to stay on mood stabilizers for their lifetime. Over time, they may be able to work with their physician to find a different dose, or combination of medications, that will lessen any side effects. But because of the nature of this disease, the likelihood of a recurrent manic or depressive episode is high. Just as people with addiction need to keep going to Twelve Step meetings, people with bipolar illness need to stay on lithium (or other similar acting medication). Even if life seems to be going very well, maintaining the program—and the prescription—keeps relapses from recurring.

Discontinuing Antidepressants

The best time to stop taking medications is when depression has let up and life is relatively stable. Even when a person is feeling well, discontinuing antidepressants during a time of turmoil may be asking too much of a brain and body to handle.

Frank was a very competent young man who had to drop out of college and return home to his parents when his depression hit. He was devastated, but started taking antidepressants and worked hard with his therapist to get back on track. Within six months, he felt like his old self again and was ready to return to school. To give himself a fresh start, he chose a different school. At the same time, he decided to stop taking his medications. He didn't tell anyone because he thought it wouldn't matter. After all, he felt better and he was embarrassed about being on antidepressants. He didn't want to risk the stigma of anyone finding out about his depression at his new school. But the combination of attending a new school, moving into a new place, and making new friends created enough stress to throw him off balance. Fortunately, Frank took quick action. He found a new therapist, got back on antidepressants, and started doing well again. There's a good chance that Frank will be able to stop taking his antidepressants soon, now that both he and his life are stable again. But this time he's not in any hurry about stopping them and wants to plan the change with his doctor.

Whether you've been on antidepressants for a relatively short time or a long time, it's best to not quit suddenly. Work out a plan with your physician to taper your medication. This means that you will take smaller and smaller doses over a period of weeks or even months. While suddenly quitting antidepressants is not life-threatening or even dangerous, it's only fair to give your body a chance to adjust to life without the medication. You may notice some physical effects of quitting medication (withdrawal symptoms), but these are generally minor and short lived. For example, some people who discontinue Zoloft or Prozac report vague feelings of "fogginess," but it soon passes. You will not experience cravings for the medication. Keep checking in with your therapist from time to time. This will give you an opportunity to continue evaluating how you are doing and diminish the chance of the depression returning.

WHAT IF I AM RECOVERING FROM ADDICTION?

If you're in recovery from addiction, it's especially important to seek help for depression for two reasons. First, the combination of depression and addiction is not uncommon, and professionals do know how to help. Second, letting the depression continue can make you more vulnerable to relapse to alcohol or drug use. Treating the depression can also help your recovery from addiction.

Some people in recovery from addiction have an erroneous belief that they should never use medications such as antidepressants. They often worry about two things. First, many people believe that Alcoholics Anonymous is against taking antidepressants because recovery from addiction and taking antidepressant medication won't work together. This is not true. In fact, antidepressants may be an important and necessary part of addiction recovery. Alcoholics Anonymous is not against antidepressants or other necessary medication prescribed by physicians and used as directed. In fact, in a pamphlet called *The A.A. Member—Medications and Other Drugs* AA members are encouraged to use medications such as antidepressants as necessary:

"A.A. members and many of their physicians have described situations in which depressed patients have been told by A.A.s to throw away the pills, only to have depression return with all its difficulties, sometimes resulting in suicide. . . . It becomes clear that just as it is wrong to enable or support any alcoholic to become readdicted to any drug, it's equally wrong to deprive any alcoholic of medication which can alleviate or control other disabling physical and/or emotional problems."[10]

Second, people in addiction recovery often worry that antidepressants may be addictive or may trigger their addiction to alcohol. This is also not true either: antidepressants are not addictive.

In this section, we will look first at stories of people who worried that taking antidepressant medication and recovering from addiction wouldn't work together. Then we will look more closely at the erroneous belief that antidepressants are addictive. Finally we will examine what is known about the effects of medication on addiction.

Medications and Alcoholics Anonymous: Can the Combination Work?

It's common for people in addiction recovery to worry about combining medication with the program of Alcoholics Anonymous. Sylvia, who has been in recovery for six years, worried about whether she could attend Alcoholics Anonymous and take antidepressants. However, she was glad she decided she could:

> *Don't listen to that inner voice that says you're a failure if you use meds. You just have to realize that when there's something wrong and there's a way to fix it, your responsibility is to fix it. Sometimes you need a little help.*

Teri also decided to take antidepressants several years after she had been in recovery. Looking back, she realized she'd been an addict since the age of sixteen and depressed since she was even younger. Her adolescence was stormy, with both addiction and depression raging within her. She finally got into addiction recovery in her late twenties, but life just didn't seem to come together for her.

I was totally drug-free for seven years. But I can't describe the depression I was in. It was totally debilitating. I can see now that it affected everything I did, all my thoughts, all my decisions. Finally I decided to get help. I still can't believe I didn't drink, drug, or kill myself. Within two weeks of being on Zoloft, for the first time in my entire life, I knew what it was like to get out of bed and face a day like a normal person. If you suffer from depression and addiction, make sure you are not self-medicating on alcohol or drugs, and get to a doctor who can help you. Depression is not your fault.

Terri fought hard for her recovery, both from addiction and depression. Because the illnesses started so early in her life, she didn't know that what she was going through wasn't the way life had to be. She was ready to accept the responsibility of being an adult and maintaining her sobriety. Terri thought that if she "white knuckled" it and tried to "grow up," she would overcome her depression. Medications helped Terry start living a life she didn't know was possible.

Some people in Twelve Step programs are fine with the idea of antidepressants, others are adamantly against it. Again, Alcoholics Anonymous, as a general organization, is not against the use of antidepressants.

Depression is not new among Alcoholics Anonymous members. In fact, the first historians who read the letters and writings of Alcoholics Anonymous' beginnings found signs of depression among members then, in the late 1940s and 1950s. Early members understood the pain and turmoil of depression, and its potential impact on sobriety. Bill Wilson, the cofounder of Alcoholics Anonymous, suffered from depression for about eleven years, between 1945 and 1955.[11] In the book *'Pass It On,'* Marty M. said, "It was awful. There were long periods of time when he couldn't get out of bed. He just stayed in bed, and Lois [his wife] would see that he ate. An awful lot of people believed he was drinking. That was one of the worst rumors we had within A.A."[12] Bill's life-long secretary, Nell Wing, said, "He would come down to the office many times and sit across from me and just put his head in his hands and really not be able to communicate, just almost weep. He used to talk about it. It baffled him."[13] She also said, "It always puzzled him, why he had to endure this suffering since, as he often said, he was so fortunate and had so much to live and be grateful for. He felt sure it must be biochemical."[14]

Bill Wilson sought help from general physicians and psychiatrists. But at that time effective treatment, either in the form of psychotherapy or medications, wasn't available. He spent time in psychoanalysis with Dr. Harry Tiebout; he went to an osteopath and cut down on sugar; he undertook a program of walking and breathing; he worked his Twelve Step program harder; he tried vitamins such as B-12 and niacin, and hormones; he even tried LSD, as a new drug of the day. Unfortunately, Bill Wilson was not able to find a treatment that could relieve his depression.

Today much more is known about depression, and many people in Twelve Step groups recognize that they have both depression and alcoholism. Here is what several people have said about how using medication and Twelve Step groups work together for them.

Chris was active in her community's Alcoholic Anonymous group, but wasn't sure how to handle the topic of taking medication.

> At first I felt very guilty about taking the medication because it went against what I was being told by some people in the program. I have talked about taking the medication at meetings since then. I wanted people to know that if a doctor diagnosed them manic-depressive, they should take the medication for their recovery, not against their recovery. I have had a couple of people walk out. This was very sad for me because then I felt that I had to hide this. For my recovery, I don't.

Gregg continued to attend Alcoholics Anonymous meetings despite the repercussions he experienced and the stigma he felt from some people in his groups when he talked about being on antidepressants. He kept in contact with his sponsor and kept applying the Twelve Step philosophy in his daily life. After a while he said:

> People in the program are beginning to be more tolerant of people with mental disorders. That's because more people are coming in the program with it. These things all help; things are changing in the program.

Most of Amy's recovery work has been in Alcoholics Anonymous, Overeaters Anonymous (OA), and Adult Children of Alcoholics (ACA). In her AA group, no one talked about depression and antidepressants. Many of her friends in OA acknowledged taking antidepressants, but it usually wasn't talked about in any detail. However, Amy found many people in her ACA group, her "safe haven," whom she felt comfortable talking to about her decision to use antidepressants and whom she could compare stories with.

How comfortable people are talking about depression and antidepressants may vary among Twelve Step groups. Amy was fortunate because she was involved in several different groups and could find the support she needed for her depression in at least one of them. All over the country, different Twelve Step groups will be more or less comfortable accepting people who are on antidepressants, depending on the region, the group members, and their shared history.

Sylvia expected her Alcoholics Anonymous group to disapprove of her use of medications. But she didn't stay away from her meetings. Instead, she discovered that the group included people she could share her story with.

> *I was surprised that I found as much encouragement at AA meetings as I did. I expected the opposite because I'd heard "no drugs whatever, for any reason" over and over again. I never believed that anyway. Even Bill W. said, "We are not doctors." I mostly know what drugs I can take, and when a doctor prescribes something for me that I don't think I should have (codeine cough syrup, for instance), I know to say thanks, but no thanks. But if I need surgery, I'll take the morphine. I don't believe that God wants us to be in pain when there is an alternative. God just wants us to use our alternatives wisely. And as my sponsor said, "If you had a broken leg, would you refuse the cast?"*

The main message is *Don't stop going to meetings.* Taking medication does not disqualify you from being a member in good standing! You may find more support and understanding than you expect. If you don't find the support you want, keep talking to your sponsor and continue to look for others in the Twelve Step program who share your story. They are there. You are not alone.

Medications and Addiction: Do Antidepressants Cause or Contribute to Addiction?

People in addiction recovery often worry that antidepressant medications are addictive. They don't want to be struggling to overcome one addiction just to replace it with another. But antidepressants are *not* addictive. As explained earlier in this chapter, antidepressants are not uppers. They do not make you happy or cheerful. A physician once pointed out that the best way to tell if a medication produces a high is to ask how much it is selling for on the street. Antidepressants clearly do not have a street market.

Many doctors use the analogy of diabetes to help people worry less about taking an antidepressant medication. Diabetics' kidneys do not produce enough insulin. An improper balance of insulin results in serious problems, including blindness, kidney failure, and loss of circulation. Although depression is not understood as well as diabetes, the same model works. For some reason it seems that people who are depressed may not be able to maintain a balance of certain chemicals in the brain. Antidepressants help the brain to regain its natural chemical balance.

LaVon was considering taking antidepressant medication, but she became afraid when her mother said she "loved" Zoloft. Using Zoloft, her mother had found freedom from a lifetime of depression. But LaVon was afraid it might be addictive. She explained how her doctor helped her see the difference between addictive and nonaddictive chemicals:

> When my mom said she loved Zoloft, it was a red flag in my mind. Although my mother has never suffered from alcohol or drug addiction, I have, and I didn't want to put myself in a position where I "loved" any kind of pills. When I mentioned this to the doctor, he asked me if I had felt good when I had used drugs in the past. I said I felt powerful, competent, and self-confident, but never "good." He pointed out that people didn't get high on antidepressants; it was just a way to overcome a chemical imbalance in your brain.

Many people who are recovering from addiction are uncomfortable with the idea of taking any kind of medication, addictive or nonaddictive. They have struggled, or may still be struggling, with adopting the mindset that life can be lived without chemicals. Even when they know that antidepressants are not addictive, they may have two feelings at the same time: one feeling is very logical, as they tell themselves, *This antidepressant is not addicting; it's a necessary and helpful medication*, and the other feeling is intense confusion.

The story of Henry shows how one recovering person decided to try medications. Henry had eight years of sobriety, was married and raising a family, and had gone back to graduate school. In spite of all the outward successes, a deep depression had tugged at Henry for as long as he could remember. Eventually, all his efforts started to unravel. His wife wanted a divorce. He couldn't find any common ground with other students at school. He felt utterly alone and had nowhere to turn for help.

> *I found myself crying frequently. I felt constantly desperate. My feeling of self-worth was gone—I was focused on my worthlessness. I felt suicidal. On Christmas Day I decided to drink first, die later. On my way to the grocery store to buy a bottle, I saw a friend from AA driving down the street. I realized that he was going to a local holiday marathon meeting. I turned my car around and followed him. When I arrived at the meeting, I told him how he had saved my life. He recommended I see a doctor in AA who is a certified addictionologist. The doctor was my family doctor when I was small, and I felt comfortable with him. I saw him the next day. He took a lengthy history and told me I had been depressed for some time.*
>
> *I don't believe I would have taken the medication if the doctor had not been in recovery. I never completely accepted the belief some people in AA hold—that a person in recovery should never take antidepressants. But I was afraid to lose my sobriety. I had seen people in the grips of withdrawal from prescription tranquilizers and wanted none of it. The doctor won my trust. He told me what to expect as possible side effects. He helped me understand that it was medication for another illness, using the insulin/diabetes model. He told me not to stop taking the antidepressant on my own, and he suggested that after I was less depressed and my life had settled down, we would decide together when I should stop.*

On the face of it, Henry's story seems like an amazing and unlikely turn of events. He was desperate, and the help he needed came in the form of an Alcoholics Anonymous friend at just the right time and place. Even more remarkable, he had the name of a physician who was not only in recovery himself and a specialist in addiction, but who was his trusted childhood family doctor. You might reasonably ask, *How could this chain of events ever be duplicated in my life?* It seems remarkably coincidental. The exact same events, in that order, will probably never happen again. But other remarkable events will occur. People recovering from addiction have many stories that seem miraculous. Somehow, when people have been on a journey of openness and self-discovery long enough, they become more able to experience help or see help in all sorts of ways they wouldn't expect. What is there to learn from Henry's story?

First, keep going to meetings. All the years that Henry went to his Alcoholics Anonymous meetings, sponsored people, and used the Twelve Step philosophy in his daily life made a difference. Many times he might have doubted that this was enough. But because he stayed on that path and kept opening himself up to change and growth, he was at the perfect time and place when he needed help. In the most fundamental way, this is spirituality at work. Whether or not you believe in God or have a relationship with a Higher Power, you can prepare yourself for this kind of remarkable coincidence.

Second, look for a physician who understands recovery from both addiction and depression.

- Henry's physician was an addictionologist. After they get their medical degree, physicians can receive a certification in addiction by completing a special course of study and passing an exam. Addictionologists understand that addiction is a disease; they also understand how to support people in their recovery. While it would be wonderful if this training was mandatory in medical school, it usually isn't. Still, more physicians are getting training in addictions. Be sure to ask your doctor about his or her experience and understanding of addiction.

- The physician was recovering. For Henry this was especially important. It was a signal to him that the doctor would understand his concerns about taking any medication. Your physician may not be in recovery or may not make that known to you. But by asking questions about your doctor's knowledge and experience, you can decide whether you are comfortable or whether you prefer to consult someone else.
- The physician was a longtime, trusted physician. In this era of health care reform, we may be often asked to switch doctors when our health care plan changes. Or we go to a clinic where we see the next doctor with an open appointment time. This makes establishing a relationship difficult. But Henry's experience points to the helpfulness of seeing a longtime physician. If you have a physician you trust, he or she might give you the assurance and direction you need about medications. However, it would have been better still if Henry's doctor was a psychiatrist. Psychiatrists have years of advanced education in emotional disorders and medications. (You may wish to refer back to chapter 4, where we looked more closely at how to choose a therapist or physician.)
- Finally, the physician spent a lot of time with Henry. He did a lengthy history. He asked questions and described what medications do and what their side effects are. He also made a commitment to work with Henry until his depression improved and he was ready to go off medications.

THE EFFECT OF MEDICATIONS ON ALCOHOLISM/ADDICTION

As pointed out several times in this chapter, antidepressant medications are not addictive. But exactly how do antidepressants affect addiction? The question really has three parts:

- Do antidepressants put you on a slippery slope toward reactivating addiction to drugs or alcohol?
- Does resolving depression increase the chance of staying sober?
- Do the same chemicals that reduce depression also reduce alcohol or drug cravings and therefore intake?

While the answers to each of these questions has been touched on earlier in the book, we will review them here.

First, do antidepressants put you on a slippery slope toward reactivating addiction to drugs or alcohol?

No research studies have found that use of antidepressant medication triggers a person's addiction. Nor are there any reports of this happening from psychiatrists or psychologists who treat addicts or alcoholics. Recovering people say that they see their two disorders as quite separate—they have an addiction and they have depression. LaVon's addiction was to "crank," an amphetamine-like drug or upper. She worried that taking antidepressants would start her down that path again. Instead she found that antidepressants affected only her depression:

> *Taking medications didn't affect my addiction—I was five and one-half years sober when I started meds, so my recovery had a life of its own. I haven't had cravings in a long time, and so far haven't relapsed.*

LaVon's addiction was stabilized with her Alcoholics Anonymous program, and the use of antidepressants didn't alter that. She was concerned about taking care of her depression. LaVon was afraid that if she became depressed again, she would isolate herself, which in turn would increase the chances of relapse to crank.

Second, does resolving depression increase the chance of staying sober?

What is the relationship between depression and relapse to drug or alcohol use? On the one hand, the two are probably so closely connected that research cannot easily untangle them. Some people know instinctively that becoming depressed is a trigger for relapse. Many of the symptoms of depression are exactly the same as the warning signs of an impending relapse. What used to be called a *dry drunk*—the negative state of mind often accompanying addiction that some people can't get out of, even though they are sober—may well be what we know today as depression. For example, many people in Twelve Step recovery are familiar with the acronym H.A.L.T., the reminder that if they get too hungry, angry, lonely, or tired, they may be setting themselves up for a relapse. The last three of those—irritability, lone-liness, and fatigue—are symptoms of depression too. A person who is depressed cannot simply decide to *not* be angry, lonely, or tired. These may be warning signs that depression is returning.

Matt recognized this and decided that the best way for him to stay on track with both depression and addiction was to think of them as two separate diseases.

> *I have to be compassionate with myself and keep in mind that I have two problems. Abstinence is critical, number one. I know that if I drink or use drugs, I can't do the work I need to do to stay not-depressed. Drinking or using drugs would keep me down. Plus, I know my therapist couldn't help me with depression if I was using. It just wouldn't work. I accept the fact that I have two diseases, and it's not my fault. Even though the depression and the alcoholism happened simultaneously, they are separate. If I fix one, the other won't automatically go away.*

Many of the same methods that help keep depression at bay fit well with reducing addiction relapses.

Third, do the same chemicals that reduce depression also reduce alcohol or drug cravings and therefore intake?

It's possible that some of the same chemical pathways in the brain are involved in both depression and addiction. Medications that balance a person's serotonin levels might correct the chemical problems that cause a person to become depressed and to use alcohol and drugs. Researchers hope that someday the neurotransmitter similarities between depression and alcoholism will be understood well enough so both can be treated with one medication. Prozac and other antidepressants are among those that are being studied for this purpose. So far, the results show some promise on a research level but less on a real-life level. For instance, there is research in which mice or monkeys are given free access to alcohol. When injected with Prozac, they drink less alcohol. Although what is true for monkeys in laboratory settings often turns out to be true for human beings, Prozac doesn't seem to make much of a difference in most people's use of alcohol. Some studies report that alcoholics on Prozac drink less at a time, or less per day, but do not necessarily achieve full abstinence.[15]

There have been some other promising studies. For example, physicians at Massachusetts General Hospital treated eight cocaine-abusing heroin addicts with Prozac. (These people weren't necessarily depressed; they were being studied just to see what effect Prozac had on their drug use.) Three dropped out of the study, saying they experienced no effect, but the other five said their cravings were reduced. Of these five addicts, three were able to become fully abstinent. However, these researchers added that some cocaine addicts report that they use more cocaine when they take Prozac; so clearly, the interactions are complex.

A few studies have been done with alcoholics who are depressed and are just beginning recovery. Typically in these studies, half the group has received Prozac and the other half a placebo. Because neither group knew whether they were receiving Prozac, their expectations should not have influenced the results. In fact, the people giving them the medications didn't even know which group was receiving Prozac. Only the researchers knew. This is the most rigorous kind of study done to test the effect of medications.

The studies found that most of the alcoholics who received Prozac experienced a decrease in depression. In addition, a small proportion of these alcoholics were able to maintain a longer period of abstinence or to have fewer drinking days.

Do antidepressants help alcoholics quit drinking? The jury is out. While it can be said with certainty that antidepressants reduce depression, no one yet knows if they help a person stay sober. It makes sense, though, that if people are less depressed, they are less likely to relapse. And it is known that decreasing depression helps people stay in a program of recovery. Perhaps this is how these medications can help both depression and alcoholism. But it is too soon to expect that antidepressant medications, in themselves, significantly alter the disease of alcoholism or addiction.

So far we have talked about whether taking antidepressants is a good idea for people who are in addiction recovery. Clearly many people benefit from their use. But if you are recovering from addiction and taking antidepressants, there are some special precautions you should know about.

Special Considerations for People Who Are In Addiction Recovery and Taking Medications

Some medications for depression or anxiety should not be used by recovering people. Some may pose risks that are intolerable to you.

If your body has been damaged by addiction, you may have to be more careful about taking antidepressants. People in addiction recovery may have liver damage or a history of seizures. Tell your physician about your health history. Some medications will not be appropriate or smaller doses will be needed with certain medical conditions.

In general, monoamine oxidase inhibitors (the category of antidepressant described in detail at the beginning of this chapter) are generally not prescribed for addicts because of their low margin of safety. Certain foods are dangerous when taking MAOIs, and people who take them must be very conscientious about strict dietary restrictions.

Finally, if you are recovering from addiction, you may be in the habit of not following directions for drug use. Sometimes recovering people recognize their tendency from their using days to think, *If one works, two will be better!* This is dangerous thinking when taking antidepressants. Be sure to follow the directions for taking your antidepressants. Antidepressants are complex chemicals and need to be taken as prescribed.

WHAT DOES THIS MEAN FOR ME?

If your therapist or someone else is suggesting that you consider taking antidepressants, keep in mind that you are in the driver's seat. Using antidepressants is not something that is done *to* you; it is something that you choose to *use* as one way to tackle your depression. It's important to be a smart consumer; you need to know (as much as possible) what to expect. You also need to be able to ask a lot of questions and to take your time in making such an important decision.

If you do decide to use antidepressant medication, feel free to ask questions of your physician. Here is a list of questions about taking antidepressants that people frequently ask. (The first five questions come from the United States Department of Health and Human Services.)[16] Your physician will probably give you this information. But this list may still be a handy review of the things you want to know as you begin taking any antidepressant.

1. When and how often do I take this medication?
2. What are the side effects of this medication?
3. Are there any foods I should not eat while taking this medication?
4. Can I take any other medication while I am taking this medication?
5. What do I do if I forget to take my medication?
6. How long will I have to take this medication?
7. What are the chances of getting better with this medication?
8. How will I know if this medication is working or not working?
9. What is the cost of this medication?
10. As a recovering person, how can I be certain this medication is not mood-altering?

After you have started taking medications, you may find you have many more questions. For instance, you may not be sure if a change you are experiencing is associated with the medication. Or you may wonder if the medication is working at all. It's important to work closely with your doctor and to ask any questions that are on your mind. Dr. Dorothy Hatsukami, a psychologist at the University of Minnesota, said:

> The thing I'd like most people using antidepressants to know is, if it's not working, or if you're having a lot of side effects, tell your doctor. I see too many people who tell me they just stopped taking their medications, or conversely, are miserable taking them. They might not realize that something can be changed—needs to be changed! It might not be the right dose or the right antidepressant.

Medications work differently for different individuals. You need to feel comfortable working in partnership with your physician to get the best combination of medication and dose.

The United States Department of Health and Human Services has five recommendations for people who are starting antidepressant medications.[17] This may be a helpful list for you to keep in mind.

1. *Keep all your appointments.* At first, your psychiatrist will ask to meet with you frequently to see how the medication is working and whether you are experiencing any side effects. After four to eight weeks if you begin to feel better, you will probably have appointments once a month or two. If you stay on antidepressants for a long period of time, you may just check in once every three months. The assumption is that you are seeing a therapist regularly and more frequently to work on problems that may underlie the depression.

2. *Ask questions.* Every medication is different. Don't assume that just because someone is a physician they can know exactly how an antidepressant medication will affect you as a unique individual. In fact, most physicians will count on you to tell them about your experience on the medication so they can make correct adjustments.

3. *Take your antidepressant as your psychiatrist tells you.* Antidepressants are complex chemicals and need to be taken as prescribed. Doses that are too high or inappropriate combinations of antidepressants can make you sick or, in rare cases, even kill you, so it is important not to change the dose or use a friend's prescription. It's also important to keep taking the medication even if you start feeling better. You should only stop taking antidepressants according to your doctor's directions.

4. *Tell your psychiatrist about any side effects you're having.* Usually, these are most noticeable during the first few weeks of taking a medication. But if you are experiencing any side effects that have you worried, don't just assume that's the way it has to be.

Call you doctor and describe what you are feeling. Changes can be made if needed.

5. *Tell your psychiatrist how the antidepressant is working.* If it isn't working, and four to six weeks have elapsed, you may need a different dose or a different medication.

FURTHER QUESTIONS

I'm in recovery and cannot take mood-altering chemicals. Since antidepressants reduce or stop depression, aren't they considered to be mood-altering?

No, antidepressants are not considered to be mood-altering. If you take a mood-altering chemical, like alcohol or cocaine, you notice a change in your mood right away. Drugs that are categorized as mood-altering have fairly rapid action, with direct effect on mood. Antidepressants do not produce any discernible change in mood in the minutes or hours after they are taken. It is only over time (days, weeks, and months) that many people taking antidepressants will notice an improvement in their depression. Antidepressants help *stabilize* a person's mood so the person can begin making changes and improvements in life. Keep in mind that antidepressants do more than affect mood; they also improve sleep, appetite, and other symptoms of depression.

Why is it okay to consider using a prescribed antidepressant when it is not okay to use other drugs that change how people feel?

Drugs that people might use on their own to alter their mood are probably addictive. For example, some people try to improve their mood by taking alcohol, cocaine, or marijuana. Initially, these might seem to work. If people are shy at a party, they may find that a drink or two makes them feel bold. Or a hit of marijuana takes the dreariness out of a dull reality. But over time, tolerance develops, and they use more and more of the chemical, trying to recapture the effects. In the meantime, preoccupation with the chemical takes on a life of its own. Alcoholism or addiction results.

Prescribed antidepressants are created to be nonaddictive. People take them under the guidance of a physician and often receive psychotherapy at the same time.

How do doctors know whether drugs are addictive or nonaddictive?

Researchers have developed several clear-cut methods for determining whether a drug is addictive. This is called *testing for abuse liability*. Here are some ways drugs are examined for their potential for dependency:

- *Drug/placebo comparison.* One group of people is given a drug and another group is given a placebo, a drug designed to look just like the drug being tested, but without effect. Neither group knows whether it is getting the actual drug or the placebo. The people being tested are given a checklist and asked to rate any physical and emotional feelings they experience. They are asked if they like the drug. In addition, researchers observe their behavior. If a drug is addictive, the group receiving it will experience changes in their feelings and they may act differently. Typically, addictive or mood-altering chemicals produce feelings of euphoria or pleasure.

- *Dose-related effects.* If a drug is mood-altering, people like more of it. The greater the dose, the greater this liking. With a placebo, it doesn't matter; a person won't feel anything different whether the dosage is small or large.

- *Animal studies.* Some types of mice and monkeys prefer alcohol or other chemicals over water or other inert substances. These animals are offered both. If they choose the drug over and over, a researcher knows the animal is discerning the mood-altering effect.

- *Withdrawal symptoms.* If a person or animal becomes physically dependent on a drug, withdrawal symptoms develop when the chemical is withheld. These symptoms include physical changes such as increased blood pressure and pulse, tremors, agitation, insomnia, and seizures. The exact nature of the withdrawal symptoms depends on the type of drug. Most drugs, if used over time, need to be discontinued slowly. The body needs to adjust to being without the chemical. What is different about mood-altering chemicals is their unique constellation of withdrawal symptoms. Someone who stops using a mood-altering chemical may have cravings, and the person may want to go back to using the drug to stop these withdrawal symptoms.

• *Tolerance.* If a drug produces addiction, people need more and more of it in order to feel its effects. This usually develops gradually, with people taking a little more to feel the euphoria or pleasure that they felt when they last used the chemical.

What kind of improvements will I notice on antidepressants?

You should notice improvements in three areas: physical, psychological, and social. Physically, you should notice that you are starting to eat and sleep better. Psychologically, you will begin to feel better about yourself and more confident. People on antidepressants do not describe this as a feeling of euphoria. Rather, they notice gradually that they are more resilient to everyday stress and do not sink as low when things go wrong. One woman said, "I didn't notice much difference at all on antidepressants, except that when I woke up to start my day, I didn't have the 'daily dreadies.'" Socially, you may begin to notice that you aren't as withdrawn. Some people on antidepressants notice that they are not as passive as they once were; they are more able to stand up for themselves.

I've been stable on meds for a period of time, but now they don't seem to be working like they used to. Can I be getting depressed again on medications?

Some people do find that a satisfactory dose loses its effectiveness over time. This does not happen to everyone. Little research has been done on this phenomenon, so it is not well understood. But psychiatrists are familiar with it and have methods of addressing it. Here are some of the most common options.

❦

Your physician might prescribe a higher dose. The following two stories show how this can work. Sarah belonged to a support group and started taking medications for her depression.

"I began at 50 mg of Zoloft . . . then a letdown . . . then went up to 100 mg and the same thing. Now I'm taking 150 mg and I've felt fine for a year

and a half. Some other women in my depression support group stayed at the lower dosage and felt okay with it even after the letdown."

Howard had a good response to medication initially but found that he, too, needed to have the dose reevaluated.

"I started off at 50 mg a day, which helped for about three months. Then I started feeling the same old feelings. I would be irritable . . . no one liked me . . . I was worthless . . . cluttered thoughts . . . obsessed with pessimistic thoughts . . . overreacting. My doctor upped my dose to 100 mg a day. I'm okay again."

You might be asked to switch to a different medication. This happens especially for people who need to be on medications for a long period of time. Over time, some people become very well attuned to their depression and their response to the medications they have received. George is truly a self-expert and needs to be because he has had so much experience with recurring depression over the course of his life. Here is his perspective.

"It's very important to know as quickly as possible when my depression is returning, because this usually means discontinuing whatever I'm taking and going to another medication for a while. Someday I hope I can find something that will work long term. With new medications being developed all the time, I think that's possible."

A small dose of another antidepressant medication might be used in addition to the one you are taking. In the 1960s and 1970s, when antidepressants were new, the accepted practice was to prescribe only one antidepressant at a time. Now it is accepted practice in some situations to use a secondary antidepressant to help the effectiveness of the main antidepressant.[18] Thirty percent of depressed people will not be helped by a particular antidepressant. Rather than give up, a physician may prescribe a small dose of another medication to use in addition to the original one. But not all types of antidepressants can be combined. It takes a skilled practitioner to know which types of antidepressants, and dosages, are safe to use together. In some cases, you may need to go off a medication for a period of time before going on a new one.

What if I can't get stabilized on the highest recommended dosage?

Don't be discouraged and don't give up! Keep going back to your physician with information about what is happening to you. There is a good chance you will find relief by changing to a different medication or a new combination of medications. Feel free to go to another physician or ask for a second opinion. There are new developments every day. And keep going to therapy and attending support groups.

What medications are most likely to be used as an adjunct to an antidepressant?

It depends on the problem. If you are taking a selective serotonin reuptake inhibitor (SSRI) such as Zoloft, Paxil, or Prozac, and it doesn't seem to be working as effectively as it could, your doctor may prescribe a small dose of desipramine or another type of tricyclic. Or your doctor may prescribe Synthroid, a thyroid hormone that improves the effect of SSRIs (B. Pepper, M.D., personal communication, 12/94). If you are experiencing anxiety, your physician may prescribe desipramine in addition to, or instead of, your usual antidepressant. If you are experiencing insomnia, you may be prescribed Desyrel.[19] However, don't be too quick to think that you need another medication until you have gotten fully stable on your original medication. Sometimes symptoms such as anxiety or insomnia may increase initially when you go on an antidepressant.

I am depressed and have an eating disorder; my doctor says that Prozac will help both. Is that true?

In April 1994, the Food and Drug Administration approved the use of Prozac for bulimia. The president of Anorexia Nervosa and Related Eating Disorders, Juean Rubel, is quoted as saying, "It isn't a magic bullet, but for the people for whom it works it's tremendous."[20] Some people with bulimia say that Prozac evens out their appetite so they do not feel such an intense need to eat large quantities of food at one sitting.

I am taking an antidepressant and I'm having insomnia; I can't fall asleep, or once I do fall asleep, I can't stay asleep.

Some medications, like Desyrel (trazodone), may be prescribed for sleep. It has a very mild antidepressant effect, which might not be enough for most people as their sole antidepressant. But its sedative effect is significant and helpful for many who are taking other antidepressants.

Should I take Xanax for my sleep problems?

No, there are two reasons why Xanax should not be taken for sleep problems. First and most important, Xanax belongs to a class of medications that is addictive, especially for chemically dependent people. Second, its powers of inducing sleep wear off over time. Then a rebound effect can occur, whereby a person has even more difficulty with sleep.

I have post-traumatic stress disorder. Will antidepressants help me?

One small study of male veterans suggests that Prozac is effective in reducing the intrusion of traumatic memories, numbing, and several symptoms of post-traumatic stress disorder (PTSD).[21] But this was a small sample. Typically, antidepressants are not used to treat PTSD unless there is an accompanying depressive disorder.

I am taking an antidepressant and I'm having problems that are sexually related.

Some people notice a loss or decrease in sexual drive on antidepressants. For men this may be particularly noticeable, since the loss in sexual drive may show up as impotence or delayed orgasm. In some cases, this can be a significant problem especially if the man is in a relationship where the couple is trying to get pregnant. For women, decrease in sexual drive may show up as difficulty in reaching orgasm or reduced sexual desire. Women may not report this difficulty, since they can still participate in sexual intercourse. Whether you are a man or a woman, if the antidepressant you are using is interfering with your ability to enjoy sexual experiences, talk to your physician.

Some people notice an increase in sex drive while taking SSRIs. This could simply be a return to normal for them if they had a decreased sex drive during their depression.

I am taking an antidepressant and I want to get pregnant. Is this okay?

In most cases, your physician will recommend discontinuing antidepressants at least during the pregnancy and perhaps through the period of time you breastfeed your child. However research is being done in this area and on occasion some antidepressants may be allowed. As this is an important, changing area, you will do best to talk to your physician about your options.

I am an elderly person. Can I use antidepressants?

Your physician will probably prescribe a lower dose than is recommended for younger people. Older adults' metabolism is generally slower, so lower doses produce the same effect. Standard adult doses in older people may produce greater side effects. However, the required dose is quite variable, so it is important to work with a knowledgeable physician. Good results with antidepressants for older people have been reported.

I am stable on medications, but have a tough time during my premenstrual phase. Is this normal? Can it be helped?

Talk to your psychiatrist about varying the dose to follow your monthly cycles. Some women find that they feel better during the premenstrual phase with antidepressants. For example, Cindy, in her thirties, reported:

> *I'm taking 50 mg a day of Zoloft. My PMS isn't as bad as it used to be. I'm not crying or angry or feeling like I hate my husband . . . yet.*

I've noticed that since starting antidepressants, I get a huge bruise when I bump into something, even lightly. Why does this happen?

In relatively rare circumstances, some antidepressants can produce changes in blood production or clotting. You should tell your doctor about the increased susceptibility to bruising.

WHAT CAN I DO TO HELP MYSELF?

1. Has a mental health professional suggested that you begin taking antidepressants? If you are considering antidepressants, what questions do you have? Make a list of your concerns. Who could you trust to answer these questions? Could you make an appointment with a psychiatrist to go over your list? You may want to get a second opinion for some questions, e.g., "Given my medical history, is this the best medication for me?" Gathering thorough, factual information may help you decide whether or not antidepressants would be helpful and safe for you.

2. If you are taking antidepressants, are you using them as prescribed? Do they seem to be working well for you? If they are not working, they might not be the right antidepressant for you. Talk to the person who prescribed your antidepressant for recommendations.

3. If you are taking antidepressants, are you also doing other things to help your depression? Many people find that therapy and other methods of self-exploration and behavior change can contribute significantly to recovery from depression; they can even help prevent future episodes.

CHAPTER 6

Depression and the Family

Psychotherapy and medication are the most important tools to use in healing from depression. But families and friends can also play a useful role—or not such a useful role—in helping people who are experiencing this illness. Peter Kramer, author of *Listening to Prozac*, concludes his book by acknowledging his family and stating, "The drug will never be invented that sustains the spirit the way a family can."[1]

When you're depressed, you usually want people to leave you alone. Yet isolating yourself can damage your relationships with friends and family. It may even seem that the relationships are not salvageable. But you can work through your depression without losing all your relationships. When you are out of your depression, you'll be glad you did what you could to keep relationships with family and friends intact.

THE IMPORTANCE OF FAMILY

If you are depressed, your family and friends can have a tremendous effect on how you feel. You may feel annoyed with them, or very dependent on them, or grateful to them, or some other feeling entirely. But it is important to remember that your illness—depression—does affect them. Of course you didn't ask to be depressed. Still, your family and friends notice that you are not yourself and they react in a variety of ways. Some will drift away. Some will flutter about you and try to give you advice. Others will not speak of their concerns because they feel awkward and confused. They don't understand what is happening to you. Some of these responses may feel helpful, some annoying. Or what feels helpful one day may feel annoying another day.

If you feel burdened by the responses of your family and friends, remember that you are not responsible for their reactions to your depression. You can be sensitive to their pain or uneasiness, but you can't change their reactions. The best you can do is to focus on your own recovery from depression. Dan could see the family dynamics around him quite clearly even though he was in the middle of his depression.

> The big danger I notice in my own family is that I can let my feelings of helplessness drive me away from being myself, or I can start expecting the impossible of myself. The truth is, my dad has helped me through this much more than my mom. My mom is so worried about doing or saying the wrong thing that I feel like I'm walking on eggshells around her. My dad doesn't do or say much, other than that he loves me and he's there for me. That's a support that's helped me more than he'll ever know.

Dan showed a tremendous amount of compassion and understanding about both his mother and his father. While he recognized that his father's reaction is most helpful, he understood that his mother is who she is, and that he doesn't need to change her or react to her.

Families can also help you as you struggle with your depression. Liz didn't believe in therapy. She was unhappy, but everyone in her family was dysfunctional so she didn't think she had much chance of being happy anyway. She figured she would just have to get through life the best she could. But watching how her sister coped with the illness helped Liz learn how to get help for her depression.

> My sister offered to take me to a therapist, but I said "no way." I refused for a year and a half as I watched her get better. It was her example of mental healing that convinced me I could get well too. I remember feeling much like Dorothy asking the Wizard, "Is there something in your bag for me?"

Sometimes families cannot help, but friends can. Their help may come in small or large ways. Noah recalled how his co-workers helped when he was depressed.

> *Sometimes at work I just couldn't hold it together anymore, and I'd go into an empty conference room and cry. I will forever be grateful to my co-workers who took time to sit with me. They didn't try to tell me what I should or shouldn't do. They didn't spread it around the office that I was having crying spells. They knew I was depressed, getting help in the best way I could, and that I wasn't going to just "cheer up." I knew they cared.*

The most important thing Noah's friends did may have been simply to sit with him. They didn't try to fix him or talk him out of his depression. William Styron, distinguished American author of several novels, had a friend who took on a more active role.

> *By the time I had commenced my autumnal plunge my friend had recovered (largely due to lithium but also to psychotherapy in the aftermath), and we were in touch by telephone nearly every day. His support was untiring and priceless. It was he who kept admonishing me that suicide was "unacceptable" (he had been intensely suicidal). . . . I still look back on his concern with immense gratitude. The help he gave me, he later said, had been a continuing therapy for him, thus demonstrating that, if nothing else, the disease engenders lasting fellowship.*[2]

Styron needed the active help his friend gave him. And in the process of giving it, his friend continued in his own recovery from depression.

WHAT DOES THIS MEAN FOR ME?

Friends and family members may be able to support you when you are going through depression, or they may not. They may react to you in ways that feel intrusive—trying too hard and being overly attentive. Or they may become angry and try to control you. How they react to your depression depends partly on them, on *their* way of dealing with difficult situations. It may also depend on you and how you interpret their reactions and their attempts to help you. It's okay to tell them how you feel about their response to you. They may or may not be able to change. But keep the door open to them as much as you can. If their concern feels off the mark now, it may be what will sustain you later. And keep looking for friends and others who will understand you.

Reaching out to people who can help you is an important part of healing from depression.

My family is trying to fix me; how can I get them to back off?

You might be feeling a little irritated by your family's efforts to help. It's natural for family members to want to help, and it's a symptom of depression to want your family to leave you alone. First, make sure you are getting help from someone—that you have at least made an appointment with a psychotherapist or psychiatrist. If you are trying to tough it out alone, your family may be giving you an important message: there is help available and it would be best to reach out and get it. Second, it's okay to tell family members that while you appreciate their concern, it doesn't feel helpful to you. Perhaps you would like people not to ask you about your depression so often, or not to give you advice. Maybe you can come to some agreement about what would feel better. Still, people are who they are and they may continue to show their concern in ways that don't feel helpful. Try not to shut yourself off from all your connections with them.

Why are my friends ignoring me?

Your friends might be ignoring you for two reasons:

1. They might feel helpless when they are around you. They can see that you're down and not doing well, but they don't know what to do about it. Feeling helpless can be scary for some people, so they may ignore you to avoid their own feelings of fear or helplessness.
2. You might (without even realizing it) have given them signals that you don't want them around. When people are depressed, they shut down emotionally and socially. In your depression, chances are you haven't been calling them or inviting them to do things. Your friends may not understand that your lack of attention toward them is due to your depression. Could you tell them that you are depressed and are not intentionally rejecting

them? This might not instantly change their behavior, but it may increase the chance that they will find some ways to be with you more.

WHAT CAN I DO TO HELP MYSELF?

1. Take a look at how your family and friends are reacting to your depression. Can you see that they may be reacting out of their own fear or misunderstanding? Are some people more comfortable with you and your depression? Remember that you can simply observe this and not try to change anybody.

2. If family and friends are not being helpful, is there a way that you can tell them what you need? They may not be able to respond as you would like, but by letting your own thoughts be known, you will have made it possible for change to occur. And you will have moved from a position of helplessness to one of some power. In depression, this can be important.

CHAPTER 7

Depression As A
Spiritual Phenomenon

Most of what people hear and read about depression implies that it is wrong, that it's bad and must be fixed—as if depression were a foreign invader, an enemy to be eliminated at all costs. Of course this illness is painful; it's not something most people would choose to experience. But there is another side to depression. For all its pain, depression can bring messages that can help people improve their lives—messages about the way they want to live, about their values, about what matters most to them.

As a society, we do not talk much about depression except in the context of new drug developments. But there are expressions of it in poetry, literature, and music—a noble, redeeming side, the side that prompts people to think deeply about life. In the depths of depression—no matter what the cause—people confront some of the most important questions that are ever asked, questions of ultimate value and purpose. Seeking the answers to these questions can help people heal from depression or avoid its recurrence.

In this way, depression can bring spiritual gifts. *Spiritual* is used here to mean the deepest parts of ourselves. People often emerge from depression having learned things that enrich their lives.

Nurturing the spirit helps to maintain emotional balance. However, please remember as you read this chapter that nurturing your spiritual life is not a substitute for getting treatment. Many people need treatment to overcome depression. All of the information you have read in earlier chapters still applies: depression is a disorder that can and should be treated.

ASKING SPIRITUAL QUESTIONS

There are problems that physicians and therapists cannot solve. This leaves people with essentially spiritual questions, the kind of questions that have many answers. And only the person asking can decide which answers fit. For instance, people with heart disease, cancer, or AIDS must ask themselves how to best live their lives in the face of persistent illness. Depression can also be chronic. Some people will need to spend a good part of their lives struggling with dysthymia, recurrent depression, or long episodes of depression. How can they best live their lives when they aren't seeing the results of their hard work toward recovery from depression? This is a question science cannot answer.

For many people, depression is relatively mild and short lived, amenable to treatment without recurrences. But as they struggle with depression, these people also find themselves asking spiritual questions.

As Judy struggled with her depression, she found herself asking such a question. Even though she seemed to have an exciting career and many friends, Judy felt numb, cut off from her feelings, and disconnected. In the depths of her depression she said:

> I have found that the deciding factor in choosing to live or die, when it comes down to that final question—and I can only speak for myself—is hope. Sometimes a glimmer is all that is needed. But sometimes even that glimmer is hard to find. If there is no hope, there is no reason for me to live.

Judy had to work hard to find reason for hope. It wasn't a question her therapist or her physician could answer for her. *Is there hope?* is a spiritual question, and Judy had to answer it for herself. But struggling with the question also helped her cope with her depression.

Asking questions about the meaning of life is often referred to as a spiritual quest or a spiritual journey. St. John of the Cross wrote about the process of the spiritual journey.[1] In his treatise he discusses "the dark night of the soul," which he describes as the bleakness of losing contact with a Higher Power. He sees this as a normal stage in the progression toward spiritual wholeness. At first, people working toward spiritual growth are filled with a sense of wholeness and fulfillment (or in his terms, closeness to God); but later they enter a period where they feel as if they have lost it all. (This sometimes happens with people working a Twelve Step program. They may come to a comfortable relationship with a Higher Power. But over time—perhaps even months or years—they feel as if they have lost the connection that sustained them in the past.) St. John of the Cross believed that walking through this night brought a person to a new and deeper relationship with God.

It is common in spiritual journeys to go through dark periods, usually after periods of progress. Being at the low point in the cycle, or dark period, can mean that your spiritual journey has taken you to a place where you are ready to face hard issues, ready to face new questions and truths. You may repeat this cycle several times.

RECOGNIZING WHEN A SPIRITUAL JOURNEY ALONE CANNOT HELP DEPRESSION

When people are in the bleak, despairing part of the cycle, they may be confused about its meanings. They may wonder if there is any point to the despair, if they are just depressed. This confusion is described in a book called *The Feminine Face of God*.[2]

> *If we have learned to trust the inner self when it sings, can we trust it when the singing goes flat or stops altogether? What is it that we trust anyway? By the time we get around to asking that question, all the beautiful and inspiring words we've read or heard or even spoken ourselves seem at best distant echoes of something we once believed. At this point, as one woman put it, "We want to know whether we're going through a 'dark night of the soul' or a depression. If it's a 'dark night,' we'll try to get through it. If not, we want Elavil."*

The fact is, people may need both antidepressants *and* a helping hand through the dark night. As noble as a spiritual quest might be, it cannot occur when people are stuck in the depths of a major depressive episode. People need to be standing on more solid ground in order to struggle with the big questions of life. Being in psychotherapy or on antidepressant medication does not stop spiritual growth. Rather, treatment can provide the solid ground that is needed to proceed with spiritual growth. It's often only when people are safely past the darkest days that they can take a step back and look at what can be learned from depression.

Some people seeking spiritual growth are reluctant or ashamed to get help for depression. They think that if they were more spiritual, meditated more deeply or longer, prayed more sincerely or often, they wouldn't be depressed. This thinking contains several fallacies.

First, depression can be an independent disorder that comes of its own accord. Yes, paying attention to spiritual aspects of life may help prevent or lessen it. Nevertheless, the disorder, like any other illness, strikes people regardless of the quality of their spiritual lives. This may seem clearer if you compare it to having an illness such as alcoholism or cancer. It doesn't make sense to think, *If I were a better person, I wouldn't be alcoholic* or *If I prayed more, I wouldn't have gotten cancer.* Nor does it make sense to think, *If I were further along on my spiritual journey, I wouldn't have gotten this depression, or at least I'd be able to get over it.* Human beings are vulnerable to various diseases. The goodness of one's soul cannot give blanket immunity. In fact, when people believe that they should be "above" getting depressed, they actually set themselves apart from the human race. As pointed out in chapter 2, depression can strike anyone.

Second, depression may be a sign of progress in a spiritual journey, rather than failure. For some people, it means that they are ready to face hard issues and feelings, perhaps ones they have been skirting for years. Until now, they may have been able to grow into competent, stable, mature adults. But further growth might not be possible until these issues are faced. Some people have buried deep grief over profound losses. Others have covered up years of abuse. Now, in their stable adulthood, they have accumulated enough inward strength—and perhaps a relationship with a higher power—to turn around and stare into the eyes of long-hidden ghosts.

Third, sometimes people look back on their lives and can see ways that depression had been present for years, but just under the surface. William Styron experienced depression later in life and reflected:

> [A]fter I returned to health and was able to reflect on the past in the light of my ordeal, I began to see clearly how depression had clung close to the outer edges of my life for many years. . . . In re-reading, for the first time in years, sequences from my novels—passages where my heroines have lurched down pathways toward doom—I was stunned to perceive how accurately I had created the landscape of depression in the minds of these young women, describing with what could only be instinct, out of a subconscious already roiled by disturbances of mood, the psychic imbalance that led them to destruction. Thus depression, when it finally came to me, was in fact no stranger, not even a visitor totally unannounced; it had been tapping at my door for decades.[3]

In some mysterious way, Styron was prepared for his depression. No one who has been through depression would ever will it again. But many people can see in retrospect how its presence made sense in their lives.

When to Get Help

How can you decide whether you are experiencing a major depression or simply a rough spot in your spiritual journey? You can use these five signs to differentiate between a spiritual crisis and a major depression:

1. You identify with many of the symptoms of major depression outlined in chapter 1.
2. You are not moving forward. You tend to your usual spiritual practices—meditation, prayer, readings, or working with a spiritual director—but you still feel stuck.
3. You have no hope.

4. You are aware, even dimly, of old grief, trauma, or losses from the past, but have not resolved or come to a comfortable place with them.

5. You are thinking of suicide.

If you are experiencing any of these five signs, you may need professional help in dealing with depression so that you can safely continue your spiritual journey. Assuming that you are willing and able to seek help for the depression as needed, let's turn to look at the ways a spiritual perspective can help during this time.

RECOGNIZING THE ROLE OF DEPRESSION

Knowing that depression can carry lessons in its wake, that it can be a path to something new, may make it easier to bear. You may even wish to ask yourself, *Does my depression have some necessary role to play?* Depression often plays a significant role in changing people's lives. Here are two images of depression that sometimes give people hope as they travel through its dark waters.

Some Spiritual Images of Depression

As a Bridge, Not an Abyss

The way you've always lived your life isn't working anymore. But you don't know how to change it, how to make things better. While you are in the midst of depression, it feels as if the misery will last forever. There seem to be no openings, no bright spots. If you can imagine this dark period of time as a bridge instead of an end point, you might feel less despair. A woman named Rose Huntley wrote about her experience:

> *When it seems that the foundations have been ripped out, those of us who experience the void feel lonely, desperate, raw, vulnerable, exposed. We may feel abandoned and a bit frantic. The old reasons do not work any more, and we cannot make them work. A friend . . . once said, "We experience the liminal place as a void, but through the power of faith we can interpret it as a bridge." This spoke to my experience.*[4]

It is telling that she uses the word *liminal*, which means "threshold." Joseph Campbell, who studied common themes in myths, uses the same idea:

> *The familiar life horizon has been outgrown: the old concepts, ideals, and emotional patterns no longer fit; the time for the passing of a threshold is at hand.*[5]

Viewing depression as a bridge, or as a threshold to another room, can require a great deal of imagination. You might feel as if depression is a deep, bottomless hole or a black wall that you can't get around. But if you can imagine it as a bridge, you can begin to see that depression is not the end.

Even when you imagine depression as a bridge, it might seem like a very long, covered bridge. You may know intuitively that your experience with depression will change your life, but you don't know what lies ahead. One of the main characteristics of depression is hopelessness about the future. So it takes courage and faith to believe that something worthwhile lies beyond the depression, even if you cannot see it or imagine it. Depression can be a bridge, a place of transition. It is not a place where you will be stuck forever.

As Transformation in the Forge

A forge can also represent depression. In Celtic religion, sacred spaces were spaces where transformation occurred, like the fiery forge or a mother's womb. The human void of suffering is also a sacred space: there is uncertainty, waiting, vulnerability, and pain. Like all transforming experiences, it is a mystery. Why do we need to experience it? What will come out of it? Theologian Shawn Madigan said:

> *The Celts sensed that forces of good spirits and bad spirits vied for power in transforming space. These vulnerable spaces bore the mystery of the impenetration of the human and the holy. Only a burning power of hope can transform the terror of the void into the promise of new life.*[6]

During depression, it can feel as if everything is dead within you. But there is work under construction. Profound internal changes are occurring. While it is sometimes impossible to be outwardly productive during depression, the psyche is continuing to move and evolve within.

As people work with depression, as they quit resisting and allow it to occur, they may discover new truths about their lives and themselves. They may also make space for new truths by letting go of things within them that have already died. Often people try to define who they are or determine their worth by external measures such as power, and they are left not knowing who they really are inside. They are left with a feeling of emptiness. If they can stop trying to fill the emptiness inside themselves with busyness or other externals, they may begin to find new ways of being fulfilled. Thomas Moore, who wrote a special section on depression in his book about the soul, says, "Melancholy thoughts carve out an interior space where wisdom can take up residence."[7] Maybe human beings need to go through phases of emptiness and pain in order to see life and themselves in new and more complete ways.

Some Spiritual Messages of Depression

Depression can indeed help people learn more about their lives. Here are some of the messages that depression may bring:

You May Need to Change Your Direction, Your Values

Depression sometimes brings the simple message that people need to change their lives. Such changes may be internal, external, or both. Often when something goes wrong, people assume that something outside needs to be changed. Instead, people may need to accept who they really are. Consider the cartoon that shows a duck standing on an psychoanalyst's couch: the psychoanalyst says, "I'm sorry, I can't help you. You *are* a duck." Who we are at the core is unchangeable. And sometimes it can take a long time to recognize, accept, and love that core self.

Once people have come to know and accept themselves, they may find that some external changes are necessary. For although the core self is unchangeable, the expression of that self in the world is changeable. In other words, people may need to make changes in the way they live so their lives better fit who they are.

After experiencing depression for almost a year, Bob started to realize he needed to make changes in his life. He had been taking antidepressant medication and had begun to feel better, but still he saw no reason for joy. Here's how he talked about his life:

> *In my thirties, I decided it was time to settle down. I got a job in a software business. It wasn't really my area of interest, but it paid well. I met a woman who wanted to get married, biological clock stuff. She wanted kids, and so did I. So we got married—for the wrong reasons, I'll admit; we never really did love each other. So now here I am, forty years old. I've lost my job and my wife is filing for divorce.*

Bob found the key to his recovery from depression when he began to see his depression as a signal that something in his life needed to change. He didn't need to simply feel better about his situation. He needed to change it or at least to allow the changes to occur. While he could improve his ability to function with medications, his depression was likely to recur unless he altered something in his life. He could cling to the belief that his job and his partner were right for him, or he could let go of that image. He could change his life to reflect who he really was by acknowledging that he was now free of a job he didn't like and a partner he had never loved. Letting go of what once seemed to fit is one of the hardest things that people are called to do in life.

People have choices as they come out of depression. They can try to patch together the remains of the life they had before, or they can make bold changes. Some people even come out of depression with renewed vigor and commitment, with a new understanding of life.

You Are Deeply Connected to the Human Race

Many truths of life seem paradoxical. For example, people who are depressed may come to understand that being absorbed in grief is an utterly lonely experience, but that it is an experience that most human beings share. Again, while people who are depressed usually feel very much alone, they may become aware of just how difficult life is for all human beings. In this way, they become aware of the bonds they share with others. For instance, you may go to the bakery counter to pick up a weekend treat, feel pleased to see a familiar woman waiting on you, and think, *She is in her forties, always there with a smile when I stop in. How can she care so much about her job? What gets her out of bed? No doubt by this time in her life she has experienced failure, been rejected, had hopes dashed, and lost people she loved. Yet somehow, she continues.* And so do you. While the reasons for each person's suffering may be unique, the fact that he or she suffers is not.

Looking back on his depression, Jim realized that there were others who understood his depair and that he needed to reach out to them.

> *I knew I needed lots of help. But I wondered,* Who can I trust? *I decided it was those who left me feeling the safest.*

You cannot overcome depression alone. You need to reach out for help. And when you reach out, you may realize that suffering is a characteristic that connects you with other human beings.

The Moment at Hand Is the Most Important

One of the great spiritual principles is to live in the moment. It is the basis of the spiritual practice of meditation. In meditation, people devote energy to focusing on the present. Becoming aware of the value of living in the present is important to healing from depression. People who are depressed typically hold a negative view of past, present, and future: *In the past I was a failure, now I am nothing, and the future holds no hope.* In fact, depression is often accidentally reinforced by taking the bleakness of today and hurling it into tomorrow. To counter this, people with depression are advised to focus just on today. The simple slogan "One day at a time" is a good reminder. And if the task at hand seems overwhelming, they need to break it down into the smallest pieces they can handle.

A Painful Childhood Can Be a Source of Strength

The depression and despair people feel as adults can stem from childhood trauma or other difficulties. When people revisit the vulnerability or devastation they experienced as children, they can become filled with despair. But the fact that they survived loss and pain as children can mean that they have special strengths that they might not otherwise have, for example, they may have learned to be especially resilient or especially sensitive to people and situations around them. While people would never ask for a painful childhood, living through such a childhood can bring gifts that help in adulthood.

Courage Matters

Depression is often described as a black cloud. As mentioned earlier, people who are depressed are generally filled with despair. Human despair, whether clinical depression or not, exists and needs to be recognized and tended to. Those who experience despair and struggle through it are courageous.

An elderly woman recalled a turning point during a particularly difficult time in her life:

> That night I thought long and not without despair about what must become of me. I wanted very much to be a person of value and I had to ask myself how this could be possible if there were not something like a soul or like a spirit that is in the life of a person and which could endure any misfortune or disfigurement and yet be no less for it. If one were to be a person of value that value could not be a condition subject to the hazards of fortune. It had to be a quality that could not change. No matter what. Long before morning I knew that what I was seeking to discover was a thing I'd always known. That all courage was a form of constancy. That is was always himself that the coward abandoned first. After this all other betrayals came easily.[8]

In the course of depression, people gain new truths about who they are. It takes courage to reclaim themselves. Depression brings the message that courage counts.

As people reach the other side of depression, they often realize that they have gained a new perspective of life. When they can step back, they realize that they see life differently, that they have grown. Zora Neale Hurston wrote:

> Well that is the way things stand up to now. I can look back and see sharp shadows, high lights, and smudgy in betweens. I have been in Sorrow's kitchen and licked out all the pots. Then I have stood on the peaky mountain wrapped in rainbows, with a harp and sword in my hands.[9]

During depression, life can seem flat and meaningless. But after depression, people look back on their lives and see how their depression affected much of what they do and who they have become. While they felt as though they were drowning, they may actually have been climbing to a new peak.

WHAT IF I AM RECOVERING FROM ADDICTION?

The Twelve Step Philosophy

The Twelve Step philosophy offers some windows into spiritual development that you can use during your recovery from depression. Before discussing these ideas, read the Steps as written from a new perspective by Lewis Andrews.

—

Step One: I have a problem that is causing me emotional distress.

Step Two: I know my Higher Power can take away my problem and restore my well-being.

Step Three: I give my problem to God.

Step Four: I look at my shortcomings as well as my good qualities as I try to cope with my problem.

Step Five: I confide these shortcomings and good qualities to another person.

Step Six: I ask myself if I am ready to have my shortcomings removed.

Step Seven: I humbly ask God to remove them.

Step Eight: As I try to cope with my problem, I acknowledge those I have harmed.

Step Nine: I [am?] thinking of how I can change my actions and directly make up for harm I have caused others.

Step Ten: Every day I continue to look at how I am doing, and when I am wrong, I promptly admit it.

Step Eleven: I take a few moments every day to seek guidance from my Higher Power.

Step Twelve: I am grateful for what I have learned from this, and I use my new knowledge and insight to help someone else.

—

Here's one way to simplify and summarize these Steps: In Steps One, Two, and Three you simply acknowledge both a need for help and a belief that help is possible. In Steps Four and Five you look inward to see if anything is preventing you from growing. In Steps Six, Seven, and Eight you build bridges with others to end your isolation. Steps Nine, Ten, and Eleven serve as reminders to "keep your house clean" so that problems will be less likely to develop. Step Twelve is a reminder to help others: most people find that reaching out to others helps them stay on solid ground.

Twelve Step philosophy contains important wisdom that can shed some light on recovery for depression. But keep in mind that working your Twelve Step program harder or better will probably not cure your depression—any more than going to psychotherapy alone cures alcoholism. Here are some ways that using the Twelve Steps can help:

Step One

Think back to how you first understood your addiction in light of Step One. Before Step One, perhaps you believed you were in complete control of your alcohol or drug use, and that it didn't affect your life very much. In listening to others, and in thinking more about your own story, you learned how Step One applied to you.

Now think about your depression. Can you see ways that depression is beyond your control? Can you begin to accept that depression has a life of its own and that it has created unmanageability in your life?

Steps Two and Three

If you are depressed, it may feel as if the weight of the world is on your shoulders. You may feel alone and without support. Whom could you turn to for help? Whom could you trust, even if just a little? There are people who care and who can help. Are you willing to turn to them?

Steps Four and Five

In the depths of depression, people can become weighed down with guilt and despair as they attempt to do a Fourth Step inventory.

When this happens, it's best to wait and work on these Steps until you are in a better state of mind. That time will come.

However, you need not avoid these Steps altogether. If you are feeling ready, doing the Fourth and Fifth Steps with your depression in mind might help you begin to see the patterns of events that keep you stuck. Some people have important inner issues that need to be aired and left behind in Step Five. But take precautions. Choose to do a "mini" Step Four and Five, looking at just a few of your characteristics and leaving the rest for another time. Set time limits: don't spend more than a half hour a day on Step Four and plan to take your Fifth Step within a week or so at most. Finally, be sure to look at some of your positive characteristics and strengths. It's just as important to acknowledge them as it is to recognize the patterns that cause you pain. In summary, plan a brief, constructive visit through Steps Four and Five this time around. When your depression is past or reduced, you'll have time and strength to do these two Steps again. In general, many people find new ways of looking at the Twelve Steps and applying them to their lives at different points in time.

Steps Six and Seven

If you are depressed, you may believe that your shortcomings are unforgivable. You might think, *I'm not the person I could've been.* Or *It's no use, I've taken all the wrong turns in life.* But these Steps are a reminder to be human and let go of the past. It may be true that you have made grave mistakes, missed opportunities, or made choices that resulted in dead ends. You may be so mired in regrets that it is hard to have hope for the moment, much less the future. You can use Step Seven as a way to focus on the here and now, and "just for today" act as the person you want to be.

Steps Eight and Nine

These two Steps are an invitation to end the isolation of depression. Whom have you shut out? Have you blamed others for your depression? Again, don't use these Steps as an opportunity to beat up on yourself. Try to keep recollections factual and simply acknowledge,

"Yes, this is what has happened." Understand that depression, as a disorder, wreaks havoc on relationships with others; just when you need people the most, depression tells you (falsely) that connecting with others is not possible. Steps Eight and Nine can help you see, with clear eyes, the impact that depression may be having on your relationships. And these Steps give you a way to reclaim those relationships. (One of the most important relationships might be with yourself.)

Step Ten

In depression, you might be tempted to analyze your whole life and put a stamp of disapproval on it. But chances are good that, if looked at more closely, your life is a mixture of noble, loving moments as well as moments of blunders and missed opportunities. Depression somehow erases the good and puts the magnifying glass on the bad. Step Ten gives you a way to look at your day—and just this day—to see what's gone well and what has gone poorly. By doing so, you can give yourself credit where credit is due. And you can give yourself a framework for noticing things you are doing that help your recovery from depression, so the next day you may be able to do a little more in that same direction.

Step Eleven

When you are depressed, your mind may feel chaotic and confused. Negative thoughts may storm inside your head. When you try to direct your thoughts, you may feel that your mind seems to go blank. Step Eleven gives you the opportunity to still your mind. You can do this by sitting quietly in a special place and, just for twenty minutes, focusing on a candle, your own rhythm of breathing, or calming music. If thoughts intrude, you can quietly acknowledge them and gently tell them to go. There is no goal in this exercise, and you may not feel an immediate benefit. But over time, you may come to realize that you have made a space for stillness within you.

Step Twelve

As you work through your depression, you may find ways to be present for others who are struggling. While this *may* help the other person, it will *most certainly* help you. By reflecting, telling someone else how it was and how it is now, you are strengthening your own position beyond depression.

Depression and Twelve Step Programs

If you have been part of a Twelve Step group, continued involvement can be critical while you are depressed. In your group, you can still find a sense of community and support. Some days it may feel too hard to get yourself there. Or you might feel that you have very little to contribute. But it's still important to go! The very same things that support your recovery from addiction will also help you in your recovery from depression.

Some Alcoholics Anonymous or other Twelve Step groups are more comfortable with depression than others. If you find that members of your group are not as compassionate as you'd like, try not to take it personally. It reflects their understanding of depression more than it does your progress in overall recovery. You may need to be selective about which group members you talk to about your depression, or you may want to shop around for a group that feels more supportive. Either way, don't give up on yourself or the Twelve Steps.

The Twelve Steps that you've become familiar with in recovery from addiction can shed some light as you travel through depression. Try looking at the Steps in new ways, as Lewis Andrews has done. Ask other people who are depressed and recovering from addiction what parts of the Twelve Step program have helped them. Again, don't fall into the trap of thinking that if you worked your program harder, you wouldn't be depressed! Be patient with yourself as you explore how you can find ways to grow in recovery from both addiction and depression.

WHAT DOES THIS MEAN FOR ME?

Depression needs to be treated, often with psychotherapy and medication. At the same time, depression may bring some important messages. Sometimes people cannot understand the messages until they are safely out of the depths of despair. But at some point, it can be helpful to reflect on what you have learned about yourself and how your life is richer for having traveled through depression.

FURTHER QUESTIONS

If I need to see a therapist or get on medication for depression, does this mean that I've failed in my spiritual quest?

No, depression is a disorder just as any other. If you developed heart disease, cancer, or a broken leg, you would probably not chastise yourself or believe that spiritual strength alone could prevent or correct these problems. Some people wait too long to get help with depression because they believe their spiritual work will sustain them or guide them through the depression. Spiritual beliefs and practices can certainly give you a guiding light, but treatment may also be necessary. Treatment for depression can actually help spiritual growth continue.

Who needs spirituality? If therapy and medication will take away my depression, why should I care about this spiritual stuff?

If treatment from depression can help spiritual growth continue, spiritual growth can also promote healing from depression. Most people who travel through depression have a profoundly changed view of themselves and their world. Finding ways to incorporate new knowledge can help people feel more solid within and more connected to their fellow human beings. In a simple way, this is spirituality.

WHAT CAN I DO TO HELP MYSELF?

Using some of the concepts of this chapter can help you see yourself and your depression in new ways. This in itself can produce movement and hope.

1. Imagine your depression as a bridge to new life and understanding. Sit with this image for a while. As you come back from your meditation, write or draw what you saw or felt. What was your bridge made of? Where did it take you? Were you alone or was someone you trusted with you? If you like, you can revisit this image anytime.

2. If you are coming out of your depression, you may be able to look back on wisdom you have gained from your experience. Take out a piece of paper, and with full respect for yourself and

your life, draw or write about some of the inner wisdom you have found.

3. In what ways have you been courageous in the face of depression? Maybe you resisted the idea of suicide. Maybe you found a way to reach out to someone else for help in spite of your fear and mistrust. Maybe you got up and out the door in the morning today even while feeling hopelessness and dread. These may be small or large victories that only you know about. But if you are surviving depression, you have been courageous.

For people in addiction recovery:

4. Which of the Twelve Steps were initially most helpful to you in your recovery from addiction? How can you apply them now to your depression?

5. Are you continuing to attend your regular Twelve Step meetings? If not, try to find ways to get yourself there. Could you call a friend and ask for a ride? Would it help to try a new meeting?

6. Is there anyone in your Twelve Step group whom you feel safe talking to about your depression? Have you talked to your sponsor about it? Would it be helpful if you did?

APPENDIX

A Brief Guide to Common Medications Used for Depression

If your doctor has prescribed a medication for your depression, you might have questions about it. This appendix gives you some basic information. Keep in mind, though, that it is only a general guide. You need to get specific, detailed information from your doctor, pharmacist, or from the written inserts that come with your medication. The most important thing this section can do is to help you understand your own questions better and give you the courage to ask them. Remember there are no dumb questions about antidepressants. Much is not known about antidepressants and how they work.

SELECTIVE SEROTONIN RE-UPTAKE INHIBITORS AND
OTHER NEWER ANTIDEPRESSANTS

Product name: Prozac
Chemical name: fluoxetine hydrochloride
How does Prozac work?
One current theory of depression says that it is caused by a deficit of the neurotransmitter serotonin, one of the brain's natural mood-enhancing chemical messengers. Prozac works by blocking the re-uptake of serotonin, leaving more serotonin available.

What are the side effects?

The most common side effects of Prozac are nausea, headaches, diarrhea, and insomnia. Nausea occurs in about 21 percent of patients; it is usually mild and subsides after a few weeks. Diarrhea occurs in about 12 percent of patients. Some people experience sexual difficulties, such as delayed orgasm; men may notice difficulty in maintaining erections.

What is the usual dose?

Typically, the initial dose is 20 mg/day, taken once in the morning. It takes six weeks to take full effect. The average effective dose is 20 to 30 mg/day; the highest recommended dose is 80 mg/day.

What about use by alcoholics/addicts?

Only a few preliminary studies have been done with alcoholics, heroin addicts, and cocaine addicts. So far, studies have found that Prozac reduces depression in most alcoholics and addicts, but has only a small effect in reducing drug/alcohol use.[1] There are no special recommendations for the use of Prozac by alcoholics or addicts.

Product name: Zoloft
Chemical name: sertraline hydrochloride

How does Zoloft work?

One current theory of depression says that it is caused by a deficit of the neurotransmitter serotonin, one of the brain's natural mood-enhancing chemical messengers. Zoloft works by blocking the re-uptake of serotonin, leaving more serotonin available.

What are the side effects?

The most common side effects of Zoloft are agitation, insomnia, ejaculatory delay, sleepiness, dizziness, headache, tremor, anorexia, diarrhea, nausea, and fatigue. Fifteen percent of depressed people given a prescription for Zoloft during studies discontinued its use due to adverse effects.

What is the usual dose?

Typically, the initial dose is 50 mg/day, once in the morning or evening. It takes several weeks to take full effect. The maximum dose is 200 mg/day.

What about use by alcoholics/addicts?

Since no specific studies have been done, there are no special recommendations for the use of Zoloft by alcoholics or addicts.

Product name: Paxil
Chemical name: paroxetine

How does Paxil work?

One current theory of depression says that it is caused by a deficit of the neurotransmitter serotonin, one of the brain's natural mood-enhancing chemical messengers. Paxil works by blocking the re-uptake of serotonin, leaving more serotonin available.

What are the side effects?

The most common side effects of Paxil are weakness, sweating, nausea, constipation or diarrhea, sleepiness, dizziness, insomnia, and problems with ejaculations. Most of these are dose-dependent; that is, the higher the dose, the more likely the side effect. Taking Paxil with food may reduce its gastrointestinal side effects. About 20 percent of people taking Paxil during its original studies discontinued use due to side effects.

What is the usual dose?

Typically, the initial dose is 20 mg/day, taken once in the morning. The maximum recommended dose is 50 mg/day. It takes two or more weeks to take full effect.

What about use by alcoholics/addicts?

Since no specific studies have been done, there are no special recommendations for the use of Paxil by alcoholics or addicts.

Product name: Desyrel
Chemical name: trazodone hydrochloride

How does Desyrel work?

The mechanism of Desyrel's antidepressant action in humans is not fully understood. It does appear to block the re-uptake of serotonin, thereby enhancing serotonin's effects. Desyrel decreases anxiety in people who are depressed and increases their sleep time. It is chemically unrelated to other antidepressants.

What are the side effects?

Drowsiness and fatigue are the major side effects of Desyrel, occurring in 20 to 50 percent of patients, especially during the first few weeks. Dry mouth is also a common side effect. Some people experience changes in sexual function, for example, a decrease or increase in libido. For men, priapism (a persistent erection) can occur. Desyrel does not cause some of the side effects that are typical of tricyclics, e.g., blurred vision, urinary retention, or constipation.

What is the usual dose?

Typically, the initial dose is 50 mg/day, taken three times/day. The maximum usual dose is 400 mg/day. It takes two or more weeks to take full effect. The dose is gradually tapered to the lowest dosage that is effective.

What about use by alcoholics/addicts?

There are no special recommendations for the use of Desyrel by alcoholics or addicts.

Product name: Effexor
Chemical name: venlafaxine

How does Effexor work?

Effexor acts on both serotonin and norepinephrine, enhancing the action of both these neurotransmitters.

What are the side effects?

The most common side effects of Effexor are short-term nausea, sleepiness, dry mouth, dizziness, constipation, nervousness, sweating, weakness, ejaculation/orgasm problems, and loss of appetite. At higher dose levels, increased blood pressure and agitation can occur.

What is the usual dose?

Typically, the initial dose is 75 to 375 mg/day. The average effective dose is usually between 125 and 150 mg/day. Some people divide it into two or three doses during the day and take it with food. It takes two or more weeks to take full effect.

What about use by alcoholics/addicts?

Since no specific studies have been done, there are no special recommendations for the use of Effexor by alcoholics or addicts.

Product name: Serzone
Chemical name: nefazodone

How does Serzone work?

Serzone appears to block the re-uptake of serotonin, thereby making the most of serotonin's effects. It is similar to Desyrel but unrelated to the other antidepressants.[2]

What are the side effects?

Nausea, headache, and drowsiness were the most frequent side effects in clinical trials of Serzone. Feelings of weakness or dizziness also appeared in a significant portion of those taking the medication. It does not have the same level of side effects as the tricyclics, making it more favorable. Overall, about 16 percent of all those involved in early trials of Serzone discontinued treatment due to side effects.

What is the usual dose?

Typically, the initial dose is 200 mg/day, taken in several doses during the day, and the usual effective dose is 300 to 600 mg/day. It takes several weeks to take full effect. The dose is then gradually tapered to the lowest dosage that is effective.

What about use by alcoholics/addicts?

There are no special recommendations for the use of Serzone by alcoholics or addicts.

TRICYCLIC ANTIDEPRESSANTS

Product name: Tofranil
Chemical name: imipramine

How does Tofranil work?

Tofranil blocks the re-uptake of several neurotransmitters.

What are the side effects?

The side effects of Tofranil may include dry mouth and eyes, blurred vision, drowsiness, constipation, sensitivity to bright light, anxiety, night sweats, weight gain, and cardiovascular problems. Men may have trouble getting an erection or ejaculating.

What is the usual dose?

Typically, the initial dose is 50 to 75 mg/day, up to 150 to 200 mg/day. It can be taken all at once during the day, or in up to four divided doses per day. It takes two or more weeks to take full effect. As soon as the depression abates, the dosage is tapered to the lowest dosage that is effective.

What about use by alcoholics/addicts?

Two studies, one in 1993 and one in 1994, were done with alcoholics. The research found that the depression improved among many of the alcoholics. For those still struggling to maintain abstinence, Tofranil seemed to be somewhat helpful in reducing drinking or relapses.

Product name: Anafranil
Chemical name: clomipramine

How does Anafranil work?

Anafranil blocks the re-uptake of several neurotransmitters. Although it is a tricyclic, it is approved in the United States for treatment of obsessive-compulsive disorder* rather than depression. Obsessive-compulsive disorder can occur with depression.

What are the side effects?

The side effects of Anafranil may include dry mouth and eyes, blurred vision, drowsiness, constipation, sensitivity to bright light, anxiety, night sweats, weight gain, and cardiovascular problems. Men may have trouble getting an erection or ejaculating.

What is the usual dose?

Typically, the initial dose is 25 to 250 mg/day, taken in several doses during the day rather than all at once. After the body becomes acclimated, one dose at bedtime suffices. It takes two or more weeks to take full effect. As soon as depression abates, the dosage is gradually tapered to the lowest dosage that is effective.

What about use by alcoholics/addicts?

Makers of the drug note that there are significant withdrawal symptoms associated with discontinuation of this medication. They point out that although drug abuse liability has not been studied, "physicians should carefully evaluate patients for a history of drug abuse and follow such patients closely."[3]

Product name: Elavil
Chemical name: amitriptyline hydrochloride

How does Elavil work?

Elavil, like other tricyclics, blocks the re-uptake of several neurotransmitters. It may help decrease anxiety in addition to reducing depression.

What are the side effects?

The side effects of Elavil may include dry mouth and eyes, blurred vision, drowsiness, constipation, sensitivity to bright light, anxiety,

---

*Obsessive-compulsive disorder is a type of anxiety disorder in which people have recurrent ideas or thoughts that interrupt their life, and/or engage in repetitive, excessive behaviors. For example, people may repeatedly check doors to see if they're locked or compulsively wash their hands. They are momentarily reassured, but then need to repeat the behavior.

night sweats, weight gain, and cardiovascular problems. Men may have trouble getting an erection or ejaculating.

What is the usual dose?

Typically, the initial dose is 50 to 200 mg/day, taken either once a day or in up to four divided doses daily. Some adults may be stabilized on 25 to 40 mg/day. It takes two or more weeks to take full effect. As soon as depression abates, the dosage is gradually tapered to the lowest dosage that is effective.

What about use by alcoholics/addicts?

There are no special recommendations for the use of Elavil by alcoholics or addicts.

Product name: Aventyl and Pamelor
Chemical name: nortriptyline hydrochloride

How does Aventyl and Pamelor work?

They block the re-uptake of several neurotransmitters and have an anticholenergic effect. They may help decrease anxiety.

What are the side effects?

The side effects of Aventyl and Pamelor may include dry mouth and eyes, blurred vision, drowsiness, constipation, sensitivity to bright light, anxiety, night sweats, weight gain, and cardiovascular problems. Men may have trouble getting an erection or ejaculating.

What is the usual dose?

Typically, the initial dose is 25 to 100 mg/day, taken either once a day or in up to four divided doses per day. It takes two or more weeks to take full effect. As soon as depression abates, the dosage is gradually tapered to the lowest dosage that is effective.

What about use by alcoholics/addicts?

There are no special recommendations for the use of Aventyl and Pamelor by alcoholics or addicts.

Product name: Norpramin
Chemical name: desipramine hydrochloride

How does Norpramin work?

It blocks the re-uptake of several neurotransmitters. It may help decrease anxiety in addition to reducing depression.

What are the side effects?

The side effects of Norpramin may include dry mouth and eyes, blurred vision, drowsiness, constipation, sensitivity to bright light, anxiety, night sweats, weight gain, and cardiovascular problems. Men may have trouble getting an erection or ejaculating.

What is the usual dose?

Typically, the initial dose is 50 to 300 mg/day, taken either once a day in the morning or at bedtime, or in up to three divided doses per day. It takes two or more weeks to take full effect. In some cases, the effect may be seen more rapidly, within two to five days. As soon as depression abates, the dosage is gradually tapered to the lowest dosage that is effective.

What about use by alcoholics/addicts?

Researchers Mason and Kocsis are doing a study to examine the effectiveness of desipramine hydrochloride in treating secondary depression (in this study, depression began after the onset of alcoholism and continued for at least three weeks after beginning abstinence). Preliminary results indicate that desipramine improves the depression and reduces relapse to alcohol.[4]

Product name: Sinequan
Chemical name: doxepin hydrochloride

How does Sinequan work?

Sinequan blocks the re-uptake of several neurotransmitters and has an anticholenergic effect. It may help decrease anxiety. It is also prescribed to help with anxiety that occurs with depression. In fact, a patient on Sinequan may feel a decrease in anxiety before experiencing a decrease in depression.

What are the side effects?

The side effects of Sinequan may include dry mouth and eyes, blurred vision, drowsiness, constipation, sensitivity to bright light, anxiety, night sweats, weight gain, cardiovascular problems. Men may have trouble getting an erection or ejaculating.

What is the usual dose?

Typically, the initial dose is 30 to 300 mg/day, taken either once a day in the morning or at bedtime, or in up to three divided doses per day. It takes two or more weeks to take full effect. As soon as depression abates, the dosage is gradually tapered to the lowest dosage that is effective.

What about use by alcoholics/addicts?

There are no special recommendations for the use of Sinequan by alcoholics or addicts.

Product name: Ludiomil
Chemical name: maprotiline hydrochloride

How does Ludiomil work?

Ludiomil appears to affect norepinephrine. It helps alleviate depression as well as anxiety. The *American Hospital Formulary* states that in studies done with Ludiomil and Elavil or Ludiomil and Tofranil, Ludiomil typically shows better results.[5]

What are the side effects?

The side effects of Ludiomil may include dry mouth, blurred vision, drowsiness, and constipation. Ludiomil may produce seizures more than other antidepressants.

What is the usual dose?

Typically, the initial dose is 75 to 150 mg/day, taken either once a day in the morning or at bedtime, or in up to three divided doses per day. It takes two or more weeks to take full effect. As soon as depression abates, the dosage is gradually tapered to the lowest dosage that is effective.

What about use by alcoholics/addicts?

There are no special recommendations for the use of Ludiomil by alcoholics or addicts.

Product name: Asendin
Chemical name: amoxapine

How does Asendin work?

Asendin blocks the re-uptake of several neurotransmitters, particularly serotonin and norepinephrine. It may help decrease anxiety that accompanies depression.

What are the side effects?

The side effects of Asendin may include dry mouth and eyes, blurred vision, drowsiness, constipation, sensitivity to bright light, anxiety, night sweats, weight gain, and cardiovascular problems. Men may have trouble getting an erection or ejaculating. This medication, in rare cases, has been associated with tardive dyskinesia, a disorder of the nervous system that is caused by long-term use of a particular psychotropic medication.

What is the usual dose?

Typically, the initial dose is 100 to 300 mg/day, taken one to three times/day. (A single dose is usually taken once daily at bedtime.) Usually it takes two or more weeks to take full effect, but for some people it works in as little as one week. As soon as depression abates, the dosage is gradually tapered to the lowest dosage that is effective.

What about use by alcoholics/addicts?

There are no special recommendations for the use of Asendin by alcoholics or addicts.

Product name: Wellbutrin
Chemical name: bupropion hydrochloride

How does Wellbutrin work?

Wellbutrin is a weak blocker of serotonin and epinephrine, and (to some extent) dopamine.

What are the side effects?

Wellbutrin appears to produce seizures at a much higher rate—as much as four times higher—than other medications. Seizures are more likely in people who have anorexia or bulimia. It also produces more weight loss than other antidepressants.

What is the usual dose?

Typically, the initial dose is 300 mg/day, taken three times/day, morning, noon, and night. It may take several weeks to take full effect.

What about use by alcoholics/addicts?

Wellbutrin "showed some increase in motor activity and agitation/excitement" and produced mild "amphetamine-like activity" among drug abusers in a research study.[6] The *Physician's Desk Reference* states that while research could not be done using higher doses (because of risk of seizures), "higher doses might be modestly attractive to those who abuse stimulant drugs." These cautions suggest that this antidepressant may not be advised for people who are recovering from addiciton—or, if it is used, patient and doctor need to make sure that low doses are being used, and any reinforcing effects are discussed.

MONOAMINE OXIDASE INHIBITORS

Product name: Marplan
Chemical name: isocarboxazid

How does Marplan work?

Marplan inhibits the enzyme monoamine, which results in the increase of several amines, including serotonin, epinephrine, norepinephrine, and dopamine. It is used for people whose depression is not helped by other antidepressants.

What are the side effects?

The side effects of Marplan may include dizziness, weight gain, and drowsiness. The most serious problem is a possible hypertensive episode, a sudden increase in blood pressure that requires emergency treatment. A headache can be a warning sign. The episode can be precipitated by eating or drinking certain kinds of food or beverages, such as aged cheese, chocolate, alcohol, or caffeine, all of which contain a monoamine called tyramine. A patient must avoid a thorough list of foods, beverages, and medications.

What is the usual dose?

Typically, the initial dose is 10 to 30 mg/day, usually taken two times a day, morning and afternoon. Doses are usually not taken at bedtime, as some people experience insomnia. It usually takes three to four weeks to take full effect. Initially, a patient might be started on the highest dose (30 mg/day) and then backed down to a lower dose. Marplan accumulates in the body, so lower doses suffice to maintain positive effects.

What about use by alcoholics/addicts?

Because of this drug's low margin of safety, it is not considered safe for alcoholics.[7]

Product name: Nardil
Chemical name: phenelzine sulfate

How does Nardil work?

Nardil inhibits the enzyme monoamine, which results in the increase of several amines, including serotonin, epinephrine, norepinephrine, and dopamine. It is used for people whose depression is not helped by other antidepressants, particularly those who have depression with anxiety.

What are the side effects?

The side effects of Nardil may include dizziness, weight gain, and drowsiness. The most serious problem is a possible hypertensive episode, a sudden increase in blood pressure that requires emergency treatment. An episode can be precipitated by eating or drinking certain kinds of food or beverages, such as aged cheese, chocolate, alcohol, or caffeine. A patient should avoid a thorough list of foods, beverages, and medications.

What is the usual dose?

Typically, the initial dose is 15 to 90 mg/day, taken two or three times a day during the morning and afternoon. Doses are usually not taken at bedtime, as some people experience insomnia. It usually takes two to six weeks to take full effect. The medication is typically started at a medium dose (three doses of 15 mg), increased until maximum effect is achieved, and then slowly tapered to the lowest dosage that is effective.

What about use by alcoholics/addicts?

Because of this drug's low margin of safety, it is not considered safe for alcoholics.[8]

Product name: Parnate
Chemical name: tranylcypromine sulfate

How does Parnate work?

Parnate inhibits an enzyme called monoamine, which results in the increase of several amines, including serotonin, epinephrine, norepinephrine, and dopamine. This MAOI produces greater stimulation than other MAOIs and takes effect more quickly.

What are the side effects?

The side effects of Parnate may include agitation, dizziness, weight gain, and drowsiness. The most serious problem is a possible hypertensive episode, a sudden increase in blood pressure that requires emergency treatment. An episode can be precipitated by eating or drinking certain kinds of food or beverages, such as aged cheese, chocolate, alcohol, or caffeine. A patient should avoid a thorough list of foods, beverages, and medications. Withdrawal symptoms, such as weakness, diarrhea, anxiety, and confusion, can also occur when it is discontinued.

What is the usual dose?

Typically, the initial dose is 30 to 60 mg/day, taken two times a day in the morning and afternoon. Doses are usually not taken at bedtime, as some people experience insomnia. It usually takes two to three weeks to take full effect. Parnate has a more complex pharmacological action than other MAOIs, and patients taking it may need to work closely with their physicians, especially at the beginning, to determine appropriate doses.

What about use by alcoholics/addicts?

Because of its special characteristics (fast-acting, stimulant effects and withdrawal symptoms), Parnate is not recommended for alcoholics or addicts. The *Physician's Desk Reference* states, "There have been reports of drug dependency in patients using doses of tranylcypromine (Parnate) significantly in excess of the therapeutic range. Some of these patients had a history of previous substance abuse."[9] Because of this drug's low margin of safety, it is not considered safe for alcoholics.[10]

MOOD STABILIZERS

Product name: lithium
Chemical name: lithium salts

How does lithium work?

Lithium is in a special category of its own and is used in treating and preventing episodes of depression and mania in people with bipolar disorder. It has the effect of reducing the wide fluctuations of mood in bipolar disorder. It can also be used to treat recurrent depression without mania. Since lithium has many complex chemical effects, how it works is not well understood. It does appear to affect neurotransmitters that are involved in depression and mania.

What are the side effects?

Lethargy, muscle weakness, fatigue, and hand tremors are the most frequent side effects of lithium. Nausea and diarrhea may also occur.

What is the usual dose?

Lithium comes in several forms (regular pills, extended release tablets, or liquid), and the dose depends on the form. Blood levels are taken when a person first begins lithium, when any changes are made, and periodically over time in order to determine whether lithium is at a therapeutic level.

What about use by alcoholics/addicts?

In the 1970s and 1980s, there was hope that lithium could be used to help alcoholics stop drinking. More rigorous research in the 1980s showed this not to be true. In most studies, use of lithium among depressed alcoholics did not decrease alcohol intake. Surprisingly, the same research showed that lithium did not improve depression among alcoholics. (However, these alcoholics were in early recovery.) Research has not been done on the effects of lithium specifically on manic-depressive symptoms of alcoholics or addicts, but it is assumed to be as effective as it is with people who are not drug dependent.

Product name: Tegretol
Chemical name: carbamazepine

How does Tegretol work?

Tegretol is useful as an anticonvulsant and analgesic, but is also effective for some people in controlling manic episodes and bipolar disorder. It may be used alone or in combination with lithium. Tegretol's most important action is to reduce some nerve cell activity in the brain ("post-synaptic")—thereby reducing seizures. But it is not known how this action produces mood stabilization.

What are the side effects?

The most serious side effects of Tegretol may include changes in the circulatory system, heart, kidneys, and liver. Although effects on these systems are not common, they can be dangerous. Because of this, it is especially important to work with a physician familiar with Tegretol and its use.

What is the usual dose?

Patients are started at a low dose and the dose is slowly increased to the most therapeutic levels. The dosage depends on the form of the drug (pills or liquid) and the nature of a patient's problems.

What about use by alcoholics/addicts?

There is no research specifically for the use of Tegretol by alcoholics or addicts.

The Twelve Steps Of
Alcoholics Anonymous*

1. We admitted we were powerless over alcohol—that our lives had become unmanageable.

2. Came to believe that a Power greater than ourselves could restore us to sanity.

3. Made a decision to turn our will and our lives over to the care of God *as we understood Him.*

4. Made a searching and fearless moral inventory of ourselves.

5. Admitted to God, to ourselves, and to another human being the exact nature of our wrongs.

6. Were entirely ready to have God remove all these defects of character.

7. Humbly asked Him to remove our shortcomings.

8. Made a list of all persons we had harmed, and became willing to make amends to them all.

9. Made direct amends to such people wherever possible, except when to do so would injure them or others.

10. Continued to take personal inventory and when we were wrong promptly admitted it.

11. Sought through prayer and meditation to improve our conscious contact with God *as we understood Him,* praying only for knowledge of His will for us and the power to carry that out.

12. Having had a spiritual awakening as the result of these steps, we tried to carry this message to alcoholics, and to practice these principles in all our affairs.

Resources

National Depressive and Manic-Depression Association
730 N. Franklin St., Suite 501
Chicago, IL 60610
Phone number: 1-800-826-3632

Depression Awareness, Recognition and Treatment Program at the National Institute of Mental Health
56400 Fishers Lane Room 14C-03
Rockville, MD 20857
Phone number: 1-800-421-4211 or 301-443-4140
This program distributes a free sixteen-page brochure titled *Depression: What Every Woman Should Know* as well as other materials.

Depressives Anonymous
198 Broadway
New York, NY 10038
Phone number: 212-964-8934

AARP Fulfillment (EE0713)
P.O. Box 22796
Long Beach, CA 90801-5796
They distribute *Backgrounder: Depression in Later Life* (D14220) and *If You're Over 65 and Feeling Depressed* (D14862)

National Alliance for the Mentally Ill
2101 Wilson Boulevard, Suite 302
Arlington, VA 22201

National Foundation for Depressive Illness, Inc.
P.O. Box 2257
New York, NY 10116
Phone number: 1-800-248-4381

Endnotes

CHAPTER 1: WHAT IS DEPRESSION?

1. American Psychiatric Association, *Diagnostic and Statistical Manual of Mental Disorders*, 4th ed. (Washington, D.C.: American Psychiatric Association, 1994), 317–93. See also *Supplement to American Journal of Psychiatry* 150, no. 4 (1993).

2. J. C. Markowitz, "Psychotherapy of Dysthymia," *American Journal of Psychiatry* 151 (8): 1114–21.

3. N. E. Rosenthal, *Winter Blues* (New York: Guilford Press, 1993) 29–39.

4. A. T. Beck, A. J. Rush, B. F. Shaw, and G. Emery, *Cognitive Therapy for Depression* (New York: Guilford Press, 1979).

5. American Psychiatric Association, *Diagnostic and Statistical Manual*, 384–86.

6. M. A. Schuckit and M. G. Monteiro, "Alcoholism, Anxiety, and Depression," *British Journal of Addiction* 83, 1373–80.

7. J. E. Helzer and T. R. Pryzbeck, "The Co-Occurrence of Alcoholism with Other Psychiatric Disorders in the General Population and Its Impact on Treatment," *Journal of Studies on Alcohol* 49 (3): 219–24.

8. C. Holden, "Depression: The News Isn't Depressing," *Science* (254): 1450–52 (1991).

CHAPTER 2: WHO HAS DEPRESSION?

1. W. Styron, *Darkness Visible* (New York: Random House, 1990); K. Cronkite, *On the Edge of Darkness* (New York: Bantam Doubleday, 1994); D. Papolos and J. Papolos, *Overcoming Depression* (New York: Harper, 1992), 4.

2. R. C. Kessler, K. A. McGonagle, S. Zhao, C. B. Nelson, M. Hughes, S. Esheman, H. Wittchen, and K. Kendler, "Lifetime and 12-Month Prevalence of DSMIII-R Psychiatric Disorders in the United States," *Archives of General Psychiatry* 51 (1994): 8–19.

3. Kessler et al., "Lifetime and 12-Month Prevalence of DSMIII-R Psychiatric Disorders in the United States."

4. D. G. Blazer, R. C. Kessler, K. A. McGonagle, and M. S. Schwartz, "The Prevalence and Distribution of Major Depression in a National Community Sample: The National Comorbidity Study," *American Journal of*

Psychiatry 151 (7): 979–86.

5. Kessler et al., "Lifetime and 12-Month Prevalence of DSMIII-R Psychiatric Disorders in the United States."

6. Kessler et al., "Lifetime and 12-Month Prevalence of DSMIII-R Psychiatric Disorders in the United States."

7. Kessler et al., "Lifetime and 12-Month Prevalence of DSMIII-R Psychiatric Disorders in the United States."

8. Blazer et al., "The Prevalence and Distribution of Major Depression in a National Community Sample."

9. P. E. Greenberg, L. E. Stiglin, S. N. Finkelstein, and E. R. Berndt, "The Economic Burden of Depression in 1990," *Journal of Clinical Psychiatry* 54 (11): 405–18.

10. H. E. Ross, F. B. Glaser, and T. Germanson, "The Prevalence of Mental Disorders in Patients with Alcohol and Other Drug Problems," *Archives of General Psychiatry* 45 (1988): 977–85.

CHAPTER 3: WHAT CAUSES DEPRESSION?

1. American Psychiatric Association, *Diagnostic and Statistical Manual of Mental Disorders*, 4th ed. (Washington, D.C.: American Psychiatric Association, 1994), 342, 348, 354, 361.

2. L. Grinspoon and J. B. Bakalar, "Depression and Other Mood Disorders," *The Harvard Medical School Mental Health Review* (1990).

3. Grinspoon and Bakalar, "Depression and Other Mood Disorders."

4. Grinspoon and Bakalar, "Depression and Other Mood Disorders."

5. J. W. Wetzel, *Clinical Handbook of Depression* (New York: Gardner Press, 1984).

6. Grinspoon and Bakalar, "Depression and Other Mood Disorders."

7. American Association of Hospital Pharmacists, *American Hospital Formulary Service Drug Information* (Bethesda, Md.: American Association of Hospital Pharmacists, 1993), 1927.

8. American Psychiatric Association, *Practice Guideline for Major Depressive Disorder in Adults* (Washington, D.C.: American Psychiatric Press, 1993).

9. American Psychiatric Association, *Diagnostic and Statistical Manual*, 717.

10. R. F. Anda, D. F. Williamson, L. G. Escobedo, E. E. Mast, G. A. Giovino, and P. L. Remington, "Depression and the Dynamics of Smoking,"

Journal of American Medical Association 264 (12): 1541–45.

11. S. M. Hall, R. F. Munoz, V. I. Reus, and K. L. Sees, "Nicotine, Negative Affect and Depression," *Journal of Consulting and Clinical Psychology* 61 (5): 761–67.

12. M. L. Parchman, "Recognition of Depression in Patients Who Smoke," *Journal of Family Practice* 33 (1991): 255–58.

13. C. Swett and M. Halpert, "High Rates of Alcohol Problems and History of Physical and Sexual Abuse Among Women Inpatients," *American Journal of Drug and Alcohol Abuse* 20 (1994): 263–72.

14. D. M. Wright and P. P. Heppner, "Coping Among Nonclinical College-Age Children of Alcoholics," *Journal of Counseling Psychology* 38 (4): 465–72; National Institute on Alcohol Abuse and Alcoholism, "Children of Alcoholics: Are They Different?" *Alcohol Alert* (Rockville, Md.: National Institute on Alcohol Abuse and Alcoholism, 1990); M. O. West and R. J. Prinz, "Parental Alcoholism and Childhood Psychopathology," *Psychological Bulletin* 102 (2): 204–18.

15. W. Coryell, G. Winokur, M. Keller, W. Scheftner, and J. Endicott, "Alcoholism and Primary Major Depression: A Family Study Approach to Co-Existing Disorders," *Journal of Affective Disorders* 24 (1992): 93–99; G. Winokur, R. Cadoret, J. Dorzel, and M. Baker, "Depressive Disease: A Genetic Study," *Archives of General Psychiatry* 24 (1971): 135–44.

16. American Association of Hospital Pharmacists, *American Hospital Formulary Service Drug Information*, 1043.

17. N. E. Rosenthal, *Winter Blues* (New York: Guilford Press, 1993) 29–39; D. A. Oren, D. E. Moul, P. J. Schwartz, C. Brown, E. M. Yamada, and N. E. Rosenthal, "Exposure to Ambient Light in Patients with Winter Seasonal Affective Disorder," *American Journal of Psychiatry* 151 (4): 591–93.

18. American Psychiatric Association, *Diagnostic and Statistical Manual*, 370–75.

19. D. G. Blazer, R. C. Kessler, K. A. McGonagle, and M. S. Schwartz, "The Prevalence and Distribution of Major Depression in a National Community Sample: The National Comorbidity Study," *American Journal of Psychiatry* 151 (7): 979–86; R. C. Kessler, K. A. McGonagle, S. Zhao, C. B. Nelson, M. Hughes, S. Esheman, H. Wittchen, and K. Kendler, "Lifetime and 12-Month Prevalence of DSMIII-R Psychiatric Disorders in the United States," *Archives of General Psychiatry* 51 (1994): 8–19.

20. S. S. Covington and J. L. Surrey, "The Relational Model of Women's Psychological Development: Implications for Substance Abuse," In *Gender and Alcohol*, ed. J. Wilsnack and R. Wilsnack (Piscataway, N.J.: Rutgers University, 1994).

21. L. S. Covey, A. H. Glassman, F. Stetner, and J. Becker, "Effect of History of Alcoholism or Major Depression on Smoking Cessation," *American Journal of Psychiatry* 150 (10): 1546–47.

22. Wright and Heppner, "Coping Among Nonclinical College-Age Children"; National Institute on Alcohol Abuse and Alcoholism, "Children of Alcoholics"; West and Prinz, "Parental Alcoholism."

CHAPTER 4: WHAT CAN I DO ABOUT MY DEPRESSION? PSYCHOTHERAPY

1. A. T. Beck, A. J. Rush, B. F. Shaw, and G. Emery, *Cognitive Therapy for Depression* (New York: Guilford Press, 1979) 386–96; G. A. Fava, S. Grandi, M. Zielezny, R. Canestrari, and M. A. Morphy, "Cognitive Behavioral Treatment of Residual Symptoms in Primary Major Depressive Disorder," *American Journal of Psychiatry* 151 (9): 1295–329.

2. D. D. Burns, *Feeling Good: The New Mood Therapy* (New York: Signet Books, 1980).

3. J. Louden, *The Woman's Comfort Book* (New York: HarperCollins, 1990).

4. W. Glasser, *Reality Therapy* (New York: Harper and Row, 1965).

5. Conari Press editors, *Random Acts of Kindness* (Emeryville, Calif.: Conari Press, 1993).

6. J. O. Prochaska, C. C. DiClimente, and J. C. Norcross, "In Search of How People Change: Applications to Addictive Behaviors," *American Journal of Psychology* 47 (9): 1102–14; J. A. Prochaska, J. S. Rossi, and N. S. Wilcox, "Change Processes and Psychotherapy Outcome in Integrative Case Research," *Journal of Psychotherapy Integration* 1 (2): 103-20.

7. Prochaska et al., "In Search of How People Change."

CHAPTER 5: WHAT CAN I DO ABOUT MY DEPRESSION? ANTIDEPRESSANT MEDICATION

1. P. E. Stokes, "Fluoxetine: A Five-Year Review," *Clinical Therapeutics* 15 (2): 216–43.

2. R. P. Greenberg, R. F. Bornstein, M. J. Zborowski, S. Fisher, and M. D. Greenberg, "A Meta-Analysis of Fluoxetine Outcome in Treatment of

Depression," *Journal of Nervous and Mental Disease* 182 (10): 547–51.

3. Stokes, "Fluoxetine: A Five-Year Review."

4. Stokes, "Fluoxetine: A Five-Year Review."

5. Stokes, "Fluoxetine: A Five-Year Review."

6. M. Konner, "Out of the Darkness," *The New York Times Magazine*, 2 October 1994, 71–73.

7. U.S. Department of Health and Human Services, National Institute of Mental Health, *Depression: What You Need to Know* (Rockville, Md.), 6.

8. U.S. Department of Health and Human Services, National Institute of Mental Health, *Depression*, 7.

9. J. F. Greden, "Understanding and Treating Major Depressive Illness," *Advances in Psychiatric Medicine*, supplement to the *Psychiatric Times*, ed. R. W. Pies (September 1994) 1.

10. Alcoholics Anonymous, *The A.A. Member: Medications and Other Drugs*, rev. ed. (New York: Alcoholics Anonymous World Services, Inc., 1994).

11. Alcoholics Anonymous, *'Pass It On,' The Story of Bill Wilson and How the A.A. Message Reached the World* (New York: Alcoholics Anonymous World Services, Inc., 1984), 292–303; N. Wing, *Grateful to Have Been There* (Park Ridge, Ill.: Parkside Publishing Company, 1992), 53–55; Alcoholics Anonymous, *As Bill Sees It: Selected Writings of the A.A.'s Co-Founder* (New York: Alcoholics Anonymous World Services, Inc., 1967), 30.

12. Alcoholics Anonymous, *'Pass It On,'* 293.

13. Alcoholics Anonymous, *'Pass It On,'* 293.

14. Wing, *Grateful to Have Been There*, 53–55.

15. R. Z. Litten and J. P. Allen, "Pharmacotherapy for Alcoholics with Collateral Depression or Anxiety: An Update of Research Findings," (forthcoming).

16. U.S. Department of Health and Human Services, Public Health Service, *Depression Is a Treatable Illness: A Patient's Guide*. April 1993. (AHCPR 93–0553).

17. U.S. Department of Health and Human Services, Public Health Service, *Depression Is a Treatable Illness*.

18. C. Holden, "Depression: The News Isn't Depressing," *Science* (254): 1450–52 (1991).

19. A. A. Nierenberg, L. A. Adler, E. Peselow, G. Zornberg, and M. Rosenthal, "Trazodone for Antidepressant-Associated Insomnia," *Archives of General Psychiatry* 151 (7): 1069–72.

20. L. McGinley, "Lilly's Prozac Is Cleared by FDA to Treat Bulimia," *Wall Street Journal,* 27 April 1994.

21. L. M. Nagy, C. A. Morgan III, S. M. Southwick, and D. S. Charney, "Open Prospective Trial of Fluoxetine for Posttraumatic Stress Disorder," *Journal of Clinical Psychopharmacology* 13 (2): 107–13.

CHAPTER 6: DEPRESSION AND THE FAMILY

1. P. D. Kramer, *Listening to Prozac* (New York: Penguin Group, 1993).

2. W. Styron, *Darkness Visible* (New York: Random House, 1990), 77.

CHAPTER 7: DEPRESSION AS A SPIRITUAL PHENOMENON

1. E. A. Peers, *Dark Night of the Soul by St. John of the Cross* (New York: Image Books, 1990).

2. R. S. Anderson and P. Hopkins, *The Feminine Face of God* (New York: Bantam Books, 1991).

3. W. Styron, *Darkness Visible* (New York: Random House, 1990), 78–79.

4. R. Huntley, "A Bridge of Faith. In *Walking in Two Worlds: Women's Spiritual Paths.* Ed. K. Vander Vort, J. H. Timmerman, and E. Lincoln (St. Cloud, Minn.: North Star Press of St. Cloud, 1991), 102–3.

5. J. Campbell, *The Hero with a Thousand Faces* (Princeton, N.J.: University Press, 1949).

6. S. M. Madigan, "Honoring the Void: Going Down and Moving Out. The Journey from Emptiness to Fullness," Theological Insights Program. St. Paul, Minn.: The College of St. Catherine.

7. T. Moore, *Care of the Soul* (New York: HarperCollins, 1992), 140–41.

8. C. McCarthy, *All the Pretty Horses* (New York: Random House, 1992) 235.

9. Z. N. Hurston, *Written by Herself,* ed. Jill K. Conway (New York: Vintage Books, 1992).

APPENDIX

1. R. Z. Litten and J. P. Allen, "Pharmacotherapy for Alcoholics with Collateral Depression or Anxiety: An Update of Research Findings," (forthcoming).

2. R. Fontaine, A. Ontiveros, R. Elie, T. T. Kensler, D. L. Roberts, S. Kaplita, J. A. Ecker, and G. Faludi, "A Double-Blind Comparison of Nefazodone, Imipramine and Placebo in Major Depression," *Journal of Clinical*

Psychiatry 55 (6): 234–41.

3. Medical Economics Data, *Physician's Desk Reference* (Montvale, N.J.: Medical Economics Data, 1994).

4. B. J. Mason and J. H. Kocsis, "Desipramine Treatment of Alcoholism," *Psychopharmacology Bulletin* 27 (2): 155–61.

5. American Association of Hospital Pharmacists, *American Hospital Formulary Service Drug Information (Bethesda, Md.:* American Association of Hospital Pharmacists, 1993).

6. Medical Economic Data, *Physician's Desk Reference* (1994) 764.

7. R. S. Schottenfeld, S. S. O'Malley, L. Smith, B. J. Rounsaville, and J. H. Jaffe, "Clinical Note: Limitation and Potential Hazards of MAOI's for the Treatment of Depressive Symptoms of Abstinent Alcoholics," *American Journal of Drug and Alcohol Abuse* 13 (3): 339–44; J. H. Jaffe, H. R. Kranzler, D. A. Ciraulo, "Drugs Used in the Treatment of Alcoholism," In *Medical Diagnosis and Treatment of Alcoholism,* ed. J. H. Mendelson and N. K. Mello (New York: McGraw Hill, 1992), 421–61; Litten and Allen, "Pharmacotherapy for Alcoholics."

8. Schottenfeld et al., "Clinical Note"; Jaffe et al., "Drugs Used in the Treatment of Alcoholism"; Litten and Allen, "Pharmacotherapy for Alcoholics."

9. Medical Economics Data, *Physician's Desk Reference,* 2266.

10. Schottenfeld et al., "Clinical Note"; Jaffe et al., "Drugs Used in the Treatment of Alcoholism"; Litten and Allen, "Pharmacotherapy for Alcoholics."

Index

A

A.A. Member—Medications and Other
     Drugs, The, 106
abuse history, 43–44, 52, 138–139
action phase of therapy, 71
addiction
     and abuse history, 43–44
     and antidepressants, 105–117, 120
     and spirituality, 146–151
     as causal factor, 37, 43–45
     diagnosis of depression in, 13–20,
          25
     prevalence of depression in, 25–26
     therapy for depression, 72–73
adolescence, 17
adoption studies, 31–32
Adult Children of Alcoholics, 43, 109
affirmations, 64
age, 25, 126
agitated depression, 13
agitation, 7, 12
alcohol, 44, 47–48, 98, 106, 116
Alcoholics Anonymous, 15, 17, 27,
          73, 105–109, 112, 114, 150, 169
alcoholism, 13, 16–17, 20, 44–45, 50,
          83, 108, 115–116, 118,
          121–122, 138–139, 148, 162
amotivational syndrome, 47
Anafranil, 158
Andrews, Lewis, 146, 150
anorexia, 97, 164
antidepressants (see specific names of
          antidepressants), 32, 42, 50, 57,
          69, 77–78, 82, 84, 98, 119, 122,
          125–127, 153, 156, 158, 162,
          164–165

and addiction, 13, 105–117, 120
and pregnancy, 126
deciding to use, 84–88, 117–118
effects on addiction, 106–117, 120
effects on individuals taking
          them, 89–91, 93
length of use, 98, 100–105
not addictive, 78, 110–111
not working, 122–125
side effects, 79, 81–83, 93, 95, 97,
          154
weight loss, 96
apathy, 8
appetite, 5
     increase in, 6
     loss of, 6
Asendin, 80, 163
atypical depression, 13
Aventyl, 80, 160

B

behavior, 57–58, 62–63, 65–66, 71, 73
bipolar disorder, 9, 23, 30, 32, 50, 84,
          104, 167–168
birth control pills, 38
blood pressure medications, 46, 52
bruises, 126
bulimia, 45, 97, 125, 164

C

Campbell, Joseph, 141
careers, 25
cause of depressions
     environment, 34–35, 44–45, 50
     genetic, 29–31, 45, 49

change, how it occurs, 64–66
chemical balance, 46
chemical imbalance, 32–33, 49–50, 111
childhood, 34–35, 43, 51, 56, 144–145
children of alcoholics, 43–44, 50
cocaine, 47
cognitive-behavioral therapy, 41–42, 56–59
compulsive overeating, 97
concentration, 7, 39, 99
contemplation phase of therapy, 70

D

Depakote, 96
depression spectrum disease, 44–45
depression vs. sadness, 61
Desipramine, 80, 124
Desyrel, 83–84, 124–125, 156
diagnosis, 6, 14
Diagnostic and Statistical Manual (1994), 39
divorce, 12, 25, 100, 111
dopamine, 78, 163–166
double depression, 9
drug withdrawal, 8
dry drunk, 114
dysthymia, 5, 9, 23–24, 69, 83, 91–92, 136

E

eating disorders, 45, 52, 83, 86, 96, 124
educational background, 24
Effexor, 83–84, 156–157
Elavil, 80, 82, 159–160, 162
endogenous depression, 10–11
environmental factors in depression, 34–35, 44–45, 50
epinephrine, 78, 163–166
estrogen replacement therapy, 40

F

family, 129–133
family history of depression, 29–31, 51
fatigue 7, 39, 46, 115. *See also* retarded depression
Feeling Good, 64
Feminine Face of God, The, 137

G

gender, 47
genetic causes in depression, 29–31, 45, 49
Glasser, William, 65
Greden, John, 103
grief, 11–12, 35–36, 41, 46, 57, 138, 140, 143
guided imagery, 64
guilt, 7, 148

H

HALT, 114–115
Halcyion, 47
Hatsukami, Dorothy, 118
helplessness, 49
Higher Power, 112, 137, 146
hormonal changes, 37–38, 40, 52
Hurston, Zora Neale, 145
hypothyroidism, 38

I

iatrogenic depression, 46
income level, 24
increase in appetite, 6
isolation, 12–13, 35, 37, 49, 65

J

Journal of Family Practice, 42

K

Konner, Melvin, 89
Kramer, Peter, 129

L

learned helplessness, 35–37
istening to Prozac, 81, 129
lithium, 84, 104, 131, 167
liver damage, 89
loneliness, 25, 35–36, 115
loss, 11, 35, 46, 51, 139–140
loss of appetite, 6
Ludiomil, 162–163

M

Madigan, Shawn, 141
maintenance phase of therapy, 71
major depression (major depressive
episode), 5–9, 12, 14, 23–24,
41–43, 68–69, 99, 139
manic-depressive illness/episode, 9, 26.
See also bipolar disorder
marijuana, 47
Marplan, 78, 164–165
marriage, 11, 25
medical illness, 8
meditation, 8, 64, 72
menopause, 40, 52
monoamine, 164–166
monoamine oxidase inhibitors (MAO
inhibitors or MAOIs), 78–79,
82, 97–99, 117, 164, 166
mood stabilizers, 78, 84, 104, 167
Moore, Thomas, 142
Morita therapy, 34

N

Nardil, 78, 165

neurotransmitters, 32, 38, 41, 46, 49,
77–80, 82, 115, 153–156,
158–161, 163
nicotine addiction, 37
norepinephrine, 32, 78, 80, 83, 156,
162–166
Norpramine, 80, 161
Nortriptyline, 96

O

obsessive-compulsive disorder, 83, 159
opiates, 47
overcompensation, 13
Overeaters Anonymous, 109
overeating, 39
oversensitivity, 13, 39

P

Pamelor, 160
panic disorder, 83
Parnate, 78, 166, 167
'Pass It On,' 107
Paxil, 81, 83, 99, 124, 155
Pepper, Bert, 99
peri-menopausal phase, 40, 52
PMS (premenstrual syndrome), 39–40
post-traumatic stress syndrome, 43,
125
postpartum depression, 38
precontemplation stage of therapy, 70
pregnancy, 38, 126
premenstrual dysphoric disorder, 39
premenstrual symptoms, 126
preparation phase of therapy, 70
primary depression, 16, 45
Prozac, 81–84, 91–92, 95, 97–98, 102,
105, 115–116, 124–125,
153–154

psychotherapy, 42, 55–56, 69, 76, 131
    and medications, 55, 75
    frequency of, 74
    length of, 69, 74

R

race, 24
Random Acts of Kindness, 66
reactive depression, 11
recovery from addiction, 2, 14, 17–18,
    25, 48, 105–106, 117
recurrence of depression, 103
relapse to drug or alcohol use, 114–117
retarded depression, 12
Rubel, Juean, 124

S

sadness, 11–13, 41, 60
seasonal affective disorder (SAD), 10,
    46, 53, 100
secondary depression, 18
seizures, 122, 162, 164
selective serotonin re-uptake
    inhibitors (SSRIs) *(see specific*
    names of SSRIs), 78, 81–82, 84,
    126, 153
self-help books, 64
serotonin, 32, 45–46, 78, 80, 82–83,
    115, 153–156, 163–166
Serzone, 83–84, 157
sexual problems, 125
Sinequan, 80, 161–162
sleep, 6–7, 10, 33, 39, 63, 97, 99, 125
sleep therapy, 34
sleeping pills *(see specific names of*
    sleeping pills), 47, 53
slowness, 7
smoking, 40–42, 48
spiritual aspects, 135–152

and Twelve Steps, 146–151
    depression as transforming,
        138–141
    need for therapy, 137–139, 151
    spiritual messages of depression,
        142–145
stress, 57
Styron, William, 23, 131, 139
suicide, 3, 8, 25, 31, 47, 61, 73, 85,
    91–92, 99–100, 106, 131, 140,
    152
symptoms of depression, 5, 9, 11,
    20–21, 42, 56, 115
Synthroid, 124

T

tardive dyskinesia, 163
Tegretol, 84, 96, 168
therapist, choosing one, 66–68
thought processes, 58–60, 62–64, 73
Tiebout, Harry, 108
Tofranil, 80, 82, 92, 95, 103, 158, 162
tranquilizers, 53
tricyclics, 78, 80–83, 94, 97–98, 124,
    158, 159
Twelve Steps, 14, 17, 67, 72, 104,
    107–110, 112, 115, 137, 146,
    150, 169
twin studies, 30–34
tyramine, 79, 165

W

weight gain, 39. *See also* appetite
Wellbutrin, 163
Wilson, Bill, 107–108
Woman's Comfort Book, The, 65
women, 38–39, 45, 48
work, 11
worthlessness, feelings of, 7, 37

X

Xanax, 47, 125

Z

Zoloft, 81, 83, 96, 100, 105, 107, 110, 122–124, 154

About the Author

Patricia Owen, Ph.D., is director of the Butler Center for Research and Education at the Hazelden Institute, part of the Hazelden Foundation in Center City, Minnesota. She holds a doctoral and master's degrees in adult clinical psychology and a M.H.A. degree in health care administration from the University of Minnesota. Dr. Owen has written numerous articles on chemical dependency issues and has given presentations at many national conferences.

Other titles that may interest you...

Today I will do one thing
Daily Readings for Awareness and Hope

This is the first meditation book for people diagnosed with dual disorders—chemical dependency and an emotional or psychiatric condition. These gentle readings help develop self-awareness, set goals, accept responsibility, and strengthen personal motivation. 400 pp.
Order No. 1400

The Dual Disorders Recovery Book
A Twelve Step Program for Those of Us with Addiction and an Emotional or Psychiatric Illness

This comprehensive recovery resource is a compelling combination of personal experience and professional insight, with real-life stories from recovering men and women plus professional contributions from noted authorities. You get an easy-to-understand look at the clinical realities of dual disorders, and a clear explanation of the relationships between psychiatric disorders and chemical dependency. 250 pp.
Order No. 1500

The Twelve Steps and Dual Disorders
A Framework of Recovery for Those of Us with Addiction and an Emotional or Psychiatric Illness
by Tim Hamilton and Pat Samples

Begin and strengthen your recovery from addiction and an emotional or psychiatric illness with the knowledge and wisdom of the Dual Recovery Anonymous program found in this book. In the tradition of *Alcoholics Anonymous, The Twelve Steps and Dual Disorders* provides an adaptation and discussion of each of the Twelve Steps of Dual Recovery Anonymous. 96 pp.
Order No. 1519

For price and order information, or a free catalog, please call our Telephone Representatives.

HAZELDEN

1-800-328-9000	1-612-257-4010	1-612-257-1331
(Toll Free. U.S., Canada, and the Virgin Islands)	(Outside the U.S. and Canada)	(24-Hour FAX)

Pleasant Valley Road • P.O. Box 176 • Center City, MN 55012-0176